Contents

Thanks and acknowledgements

The authors and publishers acknowledge the following sources of copyright material and are grateful for the permissions granted. While every effort has been made, it has not always been possible to identify the sources of all the material used, or to trace all copyright holders. If any omissions are brought to our notice, we will be happy to include the appropriate acknowledgements on reprinting.

Faber & Faber Limited, Greene & Heaton and Henry Holt & Co for the adapted text on p. 8: 'The Giordano Painting' from *Headlong* by Michael Frayn. Copyright © 1999 Michael Frayn. Reproduced by permission of Faber & Faber Limited, Greene & Heaton and Henry Holt & Co; *The Independent* for the adapted article on p. 10: 'When the hippos roar, start paddling!' by Richard Jackson, *The Independent* 10 February 1996. Copyright © Independent News & Media Limited; Telegraph Media Group for the adapted article on p. 12: 'The opera-lover turned crime novelist' by Michael White, *The Sunday Telegraph Review*, 23 March 2003; for the adapted article on p. 38: 'Fake art meets real money' by William Langley, *The Sunday Telegraph Review*, 29 June 2003; for the adapted article on p. 64: 'Lights, camera action man' by Richard Madden, *The Daily Telegraph*, 18 August 1998. Used by permission of Telegraph Media Group Limited; Jonathan Hancock for 'Picture this ... with your mind's eye' on p. 15: from *Professional Manager*, July 1998. Used by permission of Jonathan Hancock; Taylor & Francis Books Ltd for the adapted extract on p. 33: 'How useful is the term "non-verbal expression?"' from *Communicating the Multiple Modes of Human Interconnection* by Ruth Finnegan. Copyright © 2002; and the extract 'A system to notate dance' on p. 61: from *Labanotation* by Ann Hutchinson Guest. Copyright © 2005; and the adapted article on p. 93: 'Over-consumption' by Paul Wachtel from *Political Ecology*. Used by permission of Taylor & Francis Books Ltd; NI Syndication for the adapted text on p. 36: 'Chocolate Cake Wars' by Chandos Elletson, *The Sunday Times*, 22 April 2000; and the adapted text on p. 90: 'Travelling sensitively' by Mark Hodson, *The Sunday Times Travel Magazine*, 16 February 1997. Copyright © NI Syndication. Used by permission of NI Syndication; Keith Wheatley for the text on p. 41: 'Offshore Vestments' from *The Financial Times, How to Spend it*, May 1998. Used by kind permission of Keith Wheatley; Cathy Marston for the adapted extract on p. 59: 'A choreographer's diary' from www.ballet.co.uk. Used by kind permission of Cathy Marston; Rupert Wright for the extract on p. 67: 'Mazes' from *The Financial Times, How to Spend it*, October 2001. Used by kind permission of Rupert Wright; Penguin Books Ltd for the adapted text on p. 87: 'Interviewing Londoners' from *My East End, A History of Cockney London* by Gilda O'Neill (Viking Books, 1999, 2000) Copyright Gilda O'Neill 1999, 2000. Reproduced by permission of Penguin Books Ltd; Simon de Burton for the text on p. 88: 'After the Frisbee' from *Weekend Financial Times Magazine, Issue 55*. Used by kind permission of Simon de Burton; Classic FM Magazine for the adapted text on p. 99: 'How music was written down' by Jeremy Nicholas from *Classic FM Magazine*, August 2004. Used with kind permission of Classic FM Magazine.

Colour section

Alamy/Alex Segre p. C8 (b); Alamy/Blickwinkel p. C7 (b); Alamy/Chris Stock p. C12 (bl); Alamy/David R Frazier Photography p. C2 (r); Alamy/F1 Online p. C9 (b); Alamy/Image State p. C12 (tl); Alamy/Jordi Cami p. C12 (tc); Alamy/Manfred Grebler p. C12 (tr); Aamy/Mark Gibson p. C4 (tr); Alamy/Peter Steiner p. C9 (tl); Alamy/Steve Skjold p. C12 (br); Corbis/Andanson James/Sygma p. C4 (b); Corbis/Barry Lewis p. C8 (tr); Corbis/Image 100 p. C1 (tr); Corbis/Kevin Fleming p. C2 (bl); Corbis/Macduff Everton p. C10 (b); Corbis/Paul Thompson p. C12 (cl); Corbis/Roy Rainford/Robert Harding World Imagery p. C9 (cl); Corbis/Tetra Images p. C7 (t); Daniel Goodchild/Photographers Direct p. C10 (tl); Getty Images/AFP p. C5 (bl); Getty Images/AFP p. C9 (c); Getty Images/Bongarts p. C1 (b); Getty Images/Lonely Planet p. C1 (tl); Getty Images/News p. C9 (tr); Getty Images/Photographers Choice p. C9 (cr); Getty Images/Photonica p. C7 (c); Getty Images/Science Faction p. C9 (br); Getty Images/Stone p. C8 (tl); Getty Images/Taxi p. C4 (tl); Getty Images/Taxi p. C5 (br); PA Photos p. C11 (b); Punchstock/Blend Images p. C10 (tr); Punchstock/Creatas p. C11 (tr); Punchstock/Goodshoot p. C5 (t); Roger Davies/Photographers Direct p. C11 (tl); Still Pictures/Iwao Yamamoto-UNEP p. C2 (tl); United States Geological Society p. C10 (inset).

Black and white section

Alamy/AM Corporation p. 63; Alamy/Foodfolio p. 36; Alamy/Skyscan Photolibrary p. 67; Science Photo Library/Chris Butler p. 70

Cambridge Certificate in Advanced English 1

WITH ANSWERS

Official examination papers from University of Cambridge ESOL Examinations

CAMBRIDGE
UNIVERSITY PRESS

CAMBRIDGE UNIVERSITY PRESS
Cambridge, New York, Melbourne, Madrid, Cape Town, Singapore, São Paulo, Delhi

Cambridge University Press
The Edinburgh Building, Cambridge CB2 8RU, UK

www.cambridge.org
Information on this title: www.cambridge.org/9780521714426

First published 2008

Printed in the United Kingdom at the University Press, Cambridge

A catalogue record for this publication is available from the British Library

ISBN 978-0-521-714419   Student's Book without answers

ISBN 978-0-521-714426   Student's Book with answers

ISBN 978-0-521-714457   Audio CD Set

ISBN 978-0-521-714433   Self-study Pack

Introduction

This collection of four complete practice tests comprises papers from the University of Cambridge ESOL Examinations Certificate in Advanced English (CAE) examination; students can practise these tests on their own or with the help of a teacher.

The CAE examination is part of a suite of general English examinations produced by Cambridge ESOL. This suite consists of five examinations that have similar characteristics but are designed for different levels of English language ability. Within the five levels, CAE is at Level C1 in the Council of Europe's *Common European Framework of Reference for Languages: Learning, teaching, assessment*. It has also been accredited by the Qualifications and Curriculum Authority in the UK as a Level 2 ESOL certificate in the National Qualifications Framework. The CAE examination is widely recognised in commerce and industry and in individual university faculties and other educational institutions.

Examination	Council of Europe Framework Level	UK National Qualifications Framework Level
CPE Certificate of Proficiency in English	C2	3
CAE Certificate in Advanced English	C1	2
FCE First Certificate in English	B2	1
PET Preliminary English Test	B1	Entry 3
KET Key English Test	A2	Entry 2

Further information

The information contained in this practice book is designed to be an overview of the exam. For a full description of all of the above exams including information about task types, testing focus and preparation, please see the relevant handbooks which can be obtained from Cambridge ESOL at the address below or from the website at: www.CambridgeESOL.org

University of Cambridge ESOL Examinations
1 Hills Road
Cambridge CB1 2EU
United Kingdom

Telephone: +44 1223 553997
Fax: +44 1223 553621
e-mail: ESOLHelpdesk@ucles.org.uk

The structure of CAE: an overview

The CAE examination consists of five papers.

Paper 1   Reading   1 hour 15 minutes
This paper consists of **four** parts, each containing one text or several shorter pieces. There are 34 questions in total, including multiple choice, gapped text and multiple matching.

Paper 2   Writing   1 hour 30 minutes
This paper consists of **two** parts which carry equal marks. In Part 1, which is **compulsory**, input material of up to 150 words is provided on which candidates have to base their answers. Candidates have to write either an article, a letter, a proposal, or a report of between 180 and 220 words.

In Part 2, there are four tasks from which candidates **choose one** to write about. The range of tasks from which questions may be drawn includes an article, a competition entry, a contribution to a longer piece, an essay, an information sheet, a letter, a proposal, a report and a review. The last question is based on the set books. These books remain on the list for two years. Look on the website, or contact the Cambridge ESOL Local Secretary in your area for the up-to-date list of set books. The question on the set books has two options from which candidates **choose one** to write about. In this part, candidates have to write between 220 and 260 words.

Paper 3   Use of English   1 hour
This paper consists of **five** parts and tests control of English grammar and vocabulary. There are 50 questions in total. The tasks include gap-filling exercises, word formation, lexical appropriacy and sentence transformation.

Paper 4   Listening   40 minutes (approximately)
This paper consists of **four** parts. Each part contains a recorded text or texts and some questions including multiple choice, sentence completion and multiple matching. There is a total of 30 questions. Each text is heard twice.

Paper 5   Speaking   15 minutes
This paper consists of **four** parts. The standard test format is two candidates and two examiners. One examiner takes part in the conversation while the other examiner listens. Both examiners give marks. Candidates will be given photographs and other visual and written material to look at and talk about. Sometimes candidates will talk with the other candidates, sometimes with the examiner and sometimes with both.

Grading

The overall CAE grade is based on the total score gained in all five papers. Each paper is weighted to 40 marks. Therefore, the five CAE papers total 200 marks, after weighting. It is not necessary to achieve a satisfactory level in all five papers in order to pass the examination. Certificates are given to candidates who pass the examination with grade A, B or C. A is the highest. D and E are failing grades. All candidates are sent a Statement of Results which includes a graphical profile of their performance in each paper and shows their relative performance in each one.

For further information on grading and results, go to the website (see page 5).

Test 1

PAPER 1 READING (1 hour 15 minutes)

Part 1

You are going to read three extracts which are all concerned in some way with providing a service. For questions **1–6**, choose the answer (**A**, **B**, **C** or **D**) which you think fits best according to the text. Mark your answers **on the separate answer sheet**.

Fish who work for a living

Cleaner wrasses are small marine fish that feed on the parasites living on the bodies of larger fish. Each cleaner owns a 'station' on a reef where clientele come to get their mouths and teeth cleaned. Client fish come in two varieties: residents and roamers. Residents belong to species with small territories; they have no choice but to go to their local cleaner. Roamers, on the other hand, either hold large territories or travel widely, which means that they have several cleaning stations to choose from. The cleaner wrasses sometimes 'cheat'. This occurs when the fish takes a bite out of its client, feeding on healthy mucus. This makes the client jolt and swim away.

Roamers are more likely to change stations if a cleaner has ignored them for too long or cheated them. Cleaners seem to know this: if a roamer and a resident arrive at the same time, the cleaner almost always services the roamer first. Residents can be kept waiting. The only category of fish that cleaners never cheat are predators, who possess a radical counterstrategy, which is to swallow the cleaner. With predators, cleaner fish wisely adopt an unconditionally cooperative strategy.

1 Which of the following statements about the cleaner wrasses is true?

   A They regard 'roamer' fish as important clients.
   B They take great care not to hurt any of their clients.
   C They are too frightened to feed from the mouths of certain clients.
   D They are in a strong position as they can move to find clients elsewhere.

2 The writer uses business terms in the text to

   A illustrate how fish negotiate rewards.
   B show how bigger fish can dominate smaller ones.
   C exemplify cooperation in the animal world.
   D describe the way fish take over a rival's territory.

Extract from a novel

The Giordano painting

'I was up in town yesterday,' I tell Tony easily, turning back from my long study of the sky outside the window as if I'd simply been wondering whether the matter was worth mentioning, 'and someone I was talking to thinks he knows someone who might possibly be interested.'

Tony frowns. 'Not a dealer?' he queries suspiciously.

'No, no – a collector. Said to be keen on seventeenth-century art. Especially the paintings of Giordano. *Very* keen.'

'Money all right?' Tony asks.

'Money, as I understand it, is far from being a problem.'

So, it's all happening. The words are coming. And it's not at all a bad start, it seems to me. I'm impressed with myself. I've given him a good spoonful of jam to sweeten the tiny pill that's arriving next.

line 12

'Something of a mystery man, though, I gather,' I say solemnly. 'Keeps a low profile. Won't show his face in public.'

Tony looks at me thoughtfully. And sees right through me. All my boldness vanishes at once. I've been caught cheating my neighbours! I feel the panic rise.

'You mean he wouldn't want to come down here to look at it?'

'I don't know,' I flounder hopelessly. 'Perhaps . . . possibly . . .'

'Take it up to town,' he says decisively. 'Get your chum to show it to him.'

I'm too occupied in breathing again to be able to reply. He misconstrues my silence.

'Bit of a bore for you,' he says.

3 When he brings up the subject of the Giordano painting, the narrator wants to give Tony the impression of being

A cautious.
B resigned.
C mysterious.
D casual.

4 What is the narrator referring to when he uses the expression 'tiny pill' in line 12?

A his shortage of precise details about the collector
B his lack of certainty about the value of the painting
C his concerns about the collector's interest in the painting
D his doubts about the collector's ability to pay for the painting

The invention of banking

The invention of banking preceded that of coinage. Banking originated something like 4,000 years ago in Ancient Mesopotamia, in present-day Iraq, where the royal palaces and temples provided secure places for the safe-keeping of grain and other commodities. Receipts came to be used for transfers not only to the original depositors but also to third parties. Eventually private houses in Mesopotamia also got involved in these banking operations, and laws regulating them were included in the code of Hammurabi, the legal code developed not long afterwards.

In Ancient Egypt too, the centralisation of harvests in state warehouses led to the development of a system of banking. Written orders for the withdrawal of separate lots of grain by owners whose crops had been deposited there for safety and convenience, or which had been compulsorily deposited to the credit of the king, soon became used as a more general method of payment of debts to other people, including tax gatherers, priests and traders. Even after the introduction of coinage, these Egyptian grain banks served to reduce the need for precious metals, which tended to be reserved for foreign purchases, particularly in connection with military activities.

5   In both Mesopotamia and Egypt the banking systems

    A   were initially limited to transactions involving depositors.
    B   were created to provide income for the king.
    C   required a large staff to administer them.
    D   grew out of the provision of storage facilities for food.

6   What does the writer suggest about banking?

    A   It can take place without the existence of coins.
    B   It is likely to begin when people are in debt.
    C   It normally requires precious metals.
    D   It was started to provide the state with an income.

Part 2

You are going to read a magazine article about hippos. Six paragraphs have been removed from the article. Choose from the paragraphs **A–G** the one which fits each gap (**7–12**). There is one extra paragraph which you do not need to use. Mark your answers **on the separate answer sheet**.

When the hippos roar, start paddling!

*Richard Jackson and his wife spent their honeymoon going
down the Zambezi river in a canoe.*

'They say this is a good test of a relationship,' said Tim as he handed me the paddle. I wasn't sure that such a tough challenge was what was needed on a honeymoon, but it was too late to go back. My wife, Leigh, and I were standing with our guide, Tim Came, on the banks of the Zambezi near the Zambia/Botswana border. This was to be the highlight of our honeymoon: a safari downriver, ending at the point where David Livingstone first saw the Victoria Falls.

7	

Neither of us had any canoeing experience. Tentatively we set off downstream, paddling with more enthusiasm than expertise. Soon we heard the first distant rumblings of what seemed like thunder. 'Is that Victoria Falls?' we inquired naïvely. 'No,' said Tim dismissively. 'That's our first rapid.' Easy, we thought. Wrong!

8	

The canoe plotted a crazed path as we careered from side to side, our best efforts seeming only to add to our plight. This was the first of many rapids, all relatively minor, all enjoyably challenging for tourists like us.

9	

The overnight stops would mean mooring at a deserted island in the middle of the river, where Tim's willing support team would be waiting, having erected a camp and got the water warm for our bucket showers. As the ice slowly melted in the drinks, restaurant-quality food would appear from a cooker using hot coals. Then people would begin to relax, and the day's stories would take on epic proportions.

10	

One morning, Tim decided to count the number of hippos we saw, in an attempt to gauge the population in this part of the river. Most of the wildlife keeps a cautious distance, and we were assured that, safe in our canoe, any potential threats would be more scared of us than we were of them – but we had been warned to give these river giants a wide berth. They'd normally stay in mid-stream, watching us with some suspicion, and greeting our departure with a cacophony of grunts.

11	

Tim yelled 'Paddle!' and over the next 100 metres an Olympic runner would have struggled to keep up with us. The hippo gave up the chase, and although Tim said he was just a youngster showing off, our opinion was that he had honeymooners on the menu. That would certainly be the way we told the story by the time we got home.

12	

At some times of the year, you can even enjoy a natural *jacuzzi* in one of the rock pools beside the falls. The travel brochures say it's the world's most exclusive picnic spot. It's certainly the ideal place to wind down after a near miss with a hippo.

A Luckily we could make our mistakes in privacy as, apart from Tim and another couple, for two days we were alone. Our only other company was the array of bird and animal life. The paddling was fairly gentle, and when we got tired, Tim would lead us to the shore and open a cool-box containing a picnic lunch.

B If that was the scariest moment, the most romantic was undoubtedly our final night's campsite. Livingstone Island is perched literally on top of Victoria Falls. The safari company we were with have exclusive access to it: it's just you, a sheer drop of a few hundred metres and the continual roar as millions of litres of water pour over the edge.

C There was plenty of passing traffic to observe on land as well – giraffes, hippos, elephants and warthogs, while eagles soared overhead. We even spotted two rare white rhinos. We paddled closer to get a better look.

D We had a four-metre aluminium canoe to ourselves. It was a small craft for such a mighty river, but quite big enough to house the odd domestic dispute. Couples had, it seemed, ended similar trips arguing rather than paddling. But it wasn't just newly-weds at risk. Tim assured us that a group of comedians from North America had failed to see the funny side too.

E But number 150 had other ideas. As we hugged the bank he dropped under the water. We expected him to re-surface in the same spot, as the others had done. Instead, there was a sudden roar and he emerged lunging towards the canoe.

F Over the next hour or so the noise grew to terrifying dimensions. By the time we edged around the bend to confront it, we were convinced we would be faced with mountains of white water. Instead, despite all the sound and fury, the Zambezi seemed only slightly ruffled by a line of small rocks.

G When we'd all heard enough, we slept under canvas, right next to the river bank. Fortunately, we picked a time of year largely free of mosquitoes, so our nets and various lotions remained unused. The sounds of unseen animals were our nightly lullaby.

Part 3

You are going to read a newspaper article about a novelist. For questions **13–19**, choose the answer (**A**, **B**, **C** or **D**) which you think fits best according to the text. Mark your answers **on the separate answer sheet**.

The opera-lover turned crime novelist

Through her series of crime novels, Donna Leon has been solving murders in Venice with great panache – mostly to the soundtrack of grand opera.

Donna Leon first launched herself as a crime writer in 1991 with *Death at La Fenice*, which saw a conductor poisoned in mid-performance at the Venice opera house. 'It was an idea that kind of grew,' she says. 'I had a friend at the opera house. One day we were backstage, complaining about the tyrannical conductor – and we thought it would be a laugh to make him the victim in a crime novel, which I duly went off and wrote. But that's all it was meant to be. I was lucky to be born without ambition, and I had none for this book. Then I sent it off to a competition, and six months later they wrote back to say I'd won. I got a contract, and suddenly I had a purpose in life, a mission.'

To hear her talk, you'd think that until *Death at La Fenice* she'd been living in obscurity. Not so. She was a well-known academic teaching English literature at universities in the USA and Europe. But she found that she wasn't really cut out for university life, and finally decided to walk out on it. 'I'm a former academic,' she says now through slightly gritted teeth. And it's interesting that her literary reputation has been made through a medium so remote from the one she used to teach.

'You'd be surprised how many academics do read murder mystery though,' she adds. 'It makes no intellectual demands, and it's what you want after a day of literary debate.' That said, Ms Leon is big business. She sells in bulk, her books are translated into nineteen languages and she's a household name in German-speaking countries. 'All of which is gratifying for me personally, and I don't mean to rubbish my own work, but murder mystery is a craft, not an art. Some people go to crime conventions and deliver learned papers on the way Agatha Christie presents her characters, but they're out of their minds. I stay away from such events.'

Leon also stays away from most of the other expected haunts of crime writers, like courtrooms and police stations – 'I've only known two policemen, neither of them well,' – which accounts for the absence of technical legal detail in the books. What's more, the few points of police procedure that appear are usually invented – as, she admits, they're bound to be when you set a murder series in a place where murders never happen. 'Venice is small, compact, protected by its geography – there's really not much crime.' Clearly the key thing about her murder stories isn't credibility. Predictability comes closer to the mark: setting a series in a fixed location that the reader finds attractive, with a constant cast of characters.

And that's what Donna Leon does. Her unique selling point is Venice which, as the reviewers always say, comes through with such vitality and forcefulness in Leon's writing that you can smell it. There's a set cast of characters, led by a middle-aged detective, Commissario Brunetti, and his wife (a disillusioned academic). Then there are her standard jokes – often to do with food. Indeed, Leon lingers so ecstatically over the details of lunch, the pursuit of justice frequently gets diverted. The eating is a literary device – part of the pattern of each novel, into which she slots the plot. 'That's how you hook your readers, who like a kind of certainty. And the most attractive certainty of crime fiction is that it gives them what real life doesn't. The bad guy gets it in the end.'

Indeed, when the conversation switches to Donna Leon's other life, *Il Complesso Barocco*, the opera company she helps run, she talks about baroque opera as though it were murder-mystery: fuelled by 'power, jealousy and rage, despair, menace' which are her own words for the sleeve notes of a new CD of Handel arias by the company, packaged under the title *The Abandoned Sorceress*. Designed to tour rare works in concert format, *Il Complesso* was set up in 2001 in collaboration with another US exile in Italy, the musicologist Alan Curtis. 'It started as a one-off. There was a rare Handel opera, *Arminio*, that Alan thought should be performed, and it became an obsession for him until eventually I said, 'Do you want to talk about this or do you want to do it?' So we did it. I rang a friend who runs a Swiss opera festival. We offered him a production. Then had eight months to get it together.'

Somehow it came together, and *Il Complesso* is now an ongoing venture. Curtis does the hands-on artistic and administrative work. Leon lends her name which 'opens doors in all those German-speaking places' and, crucially, underwrites the costs. In addition, her publishing commitments take her all over Europe – where she keeps a lookout for potential singers, and sometimes even features in the productions herself: not singing ('I don't') but reading the odd snatch from her books.

13 What is suggested about the novel *Death at La Fenice* in the first paragraph?

  A Donna based the plot on a real-life event she had witnessed.
  B Donna didn't envisage the work ever being taken very seriously.
  C Donna had to be persuaded that it was good enough to win a prize.
  D Donna embarked upon it as a way of bringing about a change in her life.

14 The second paragraph paints a picture of Donna as someone who

  A has little respect for her fellow academics.
  B regrets having given up her job in a university.
  C was unsuited to being a university teacher.
  D failed to make a success of her academic career.

15 From Donna's comments in the third paragraph, we understand that

  A she feels crime fiction should be considered alongside other types of literature.
  B she is pleased with the level of recognition that her own novels have received.
  C she regards her own novels as inferior to those of Agatha Christie.
  D she finds the popularity of crime novels amongst academics very satisfying.

16 Donna is described as an untypical crime writer because

  A she is able to imagine crimes being committed by unlikely characters.
  B she is unconcerned whether or not her stories appear realistic.
  C she has little interest in the ways criminals think and operate.
  D she manages to come up with imaginative new ideas for her plots.

17 Donna's greatest strength as a crime writer is seen as

  A her avoidance of a fixed approach.
  B her injection of humour into her stories.
  C the clear moral message she puts across.
  D the strong evocation of place she achieves.

18 When Donna helped set up *Il Complesso Barocco,*

  A she didn't expect it to be a long-term project.
  B she saw it as more interesting than her writing work.
  C she had a fundamental disagreement with her main collaborator.
  D she was attracted by the challenge of the first deadline.

19 In what way is Donna important to *Il Complesso Barocco*?

  A She provides essential financial support.
  B She oversees its day-to-day organisation.
  C She helps as a translator.
  D She organises the recruitment of performers.

Part 4

You are going to read an article about the human mind. For questions **20–34,** choose from the sections (**A–E**). The sections may be chosen more than once.

Mark your answers **on the separate answer sheet**.

Which section mentions the following?

things that you will not need if you adopt a certain mental technique	**20**
using an image of a familiar place to help you remember things	**21**
being able to think about both particular points and general points	**22**
things that you may not have a clear mental picture of	**23**
something which appears to be disorganised	**24**
annoyance at your inability to remember things	**25**
bearing in mind what you want to achieve in the future	**26**
an example of an industry in which people use pictures effectively	**27**
an everyday example of failure to keep information in the mind	**28**
the impact a certain mental technique can have on people listening to what you say	**29**
an assertion that certain things can be kept in your mind more easily than others	**30**
information that it is essential to recall in certain situations	**31**
being able to consider things from various points of view	**32**
things that come into your mind in an illogical sequence	**33**
remembering written work by imagining it in context	**34**

Picture this ... with your mind's eye

Trying to understand and cope with life, we impose our own frameworks on it and represent information in different symbolic forms in our mind, writes Jonathan Hancock.

A

Think of the mental maps you use to find your way around the places you live and work. Which way up do you picture towns and cities you know well? Which details are highlighted, which ones blurred? Just as the map of London used by passengers on the Underground is different from the one used by drivers above ground, so your mental framework differs from that of other people. We also use frameworks to organise more abstract information. Many people say that they can visualise the position of key passages in books or documents. Mention a point made by the author, and they can recall and respond to it by picturing it in relation to other key points within the larger framework they see in their mind's eye. On a chaotic-looking desk, it is often possible to see a mental picture of where the key pieces of paper are and find a particular document in seconds.

B

We all have our own natural strategies for structuring information, for altering and re-arranging it in our mind's eye. You can take control of your thinking by increasing your control of the mental frameworks you create. Since Ancient Roman times, a specific framing technique has been used to improve memory and boost clarity of thought. The concept is simple: you design an empty framework, based on the shape of a building you know well, and get used to moving around its rooms and hallways in your mind. Whenever you have information to remember, you place it in this 'virtual storehouse'. Whatever it is you are learning – words, numbers, names, jobs, ideas – you invent pictorial clues to represent each one. The mind prefers images to abstract ideas, and can retain vast numbers of visual clues. Just as advertisers bring concepts to life with key images, you highlight the important points in a batch of information and assign each of them an illustration.

C

Memory and place are closely linked. Have you ever walked upstairs, forgotten what you went for, but remembered when you returned to where you were standing when you first had the thought? When you are trying to learn new information, it makes sense to use the mind's natural tendencies. In your mind, you return to the imaginary rooms in your 'virtual storehouse', and rediscover the images you left there. Cicero, perhaps the greatest orator in history, is reputed to have used this technique to recall complex legal arguments, addressing the Roman Senate from memory for days on end. You can use it to remember all the employees in your new workplace, the jobs you have to do in a day, month or year, subject headings for a complex piece of work, or the facts you need to have at your fingertips under pressurised circumstances.

D

The system of combining images and ideas works so well because it involves 'global thinking', bringing together the two 'sides' of your brain. The left side governs logic, words, numbers, patterns and structured thought – the frameworks you build – and the right side works on random thoughts, pictures, daydreams – the memorable imagery you fill them with. The fearless, imaginative creativity of the child combines with the patterning, prioritising, structured thinking of the adult. The memory is activated with colours and feelings, as you create weird, funny, exciting, surreal scenes; and the information is kept under control by the organised frameworks you design. Imagination is the key. You enter a new dimension, dealing with information in a form that suits the way the mind works. In this accessible form, huge amounts of data can be carried around with you. You never again have to search around for an address book, diary or telephone number on a scrap of paper. Your memory becomes a key part of your success, rather than the thing you curse as the cause of your failure.

E

Bringing information into the field of your imagination helps you to explore it in greater depth and from different angles. Storing it in the frameworks of your mind allows you to pick out key details but also to see the big picture. You can use your trained memory to organise your life: to see the day-to-day facts and figures, names, times and dates, but also to keep in touch with your long-term goals. By understanding the way your mind works, you can make yourself memorable to others. Give your thoughts a shape and structure that can be grasped and others will remember what you have to say. You can take your imaginative grasp of the world to a new level and, by making the most of mental frames, you can put the information you need at your disposal more readily.

PAPER 2   WRITING (1 hour 30 minutes)

Part 1

You **must** answer this question. Write your answer in **180–220** words in an appropriate style.

---

1   You are studying at a college in Canada. Recently you and some other students attended a two-day Careers Conference. As the college paid for you, the College Principal has asked you to write a report about the conference. You and the other students have discussed the conference and you have made notes on their views.

Read the conference programme together with your notes below. Then, **using the information appropriately**, write a report for the Principal explaining how useful the conference was and making recommendations for next year.

> **CAREERS CONFERENCE**
>
> Vancouver Hall
> Friday – Sunday, 9am–6pm
> Exhibition – over 100 different jobs
> Talks on wide range of careers
> Experts available to give advice

Notes on students' views:

- *exhibition great*

- *some talks good*

- *not enough people to answer questions*

- *better for science students than e.g. language or history students*

Now write your **report** for the College Principal, as outlined above. You should use your own words as far as possible.

Part 2

Choose **one** of the following writing tasks. Your answer should follow exactly the instructions given. Write approximately **220–260** words.

2   You have seen the following announcement in an international magazine.

> ### FASHION AND CHANGING LIFESTYLES
>
> Do you think that fashion reflects changes in how people live? We would like to know how fashion in clothes has changed since your grandparents were young, and what this reveals about changes in society in your country.
>
> The most interesting articles will be published in the next issue of our magazine.

Write your **article**.

3   An English-speaking friend is writing a book on TV programmes in different countries. Your friend has asked you for a contribution about the most popular TV programme in your country. Your contribution should:

- briefly describe the most popular TV programme
- explain why the programme is so popular
- explain whether or not you think it deserves its popularity.

Write your **contribution** to the book.

4   You see this notice in the local library of the town where you are studying English.

> The *International Development Agency* has given our town a grant to be spent on improving transport and housing facilities.
>
> The Planning Director invites you to send a proposal outlining any problems with existing transport **and** housing facilities and explaining how they can be improved. A decision can then be made about how the money should be spent.

Write your **proposal**.

5   Answer **one** of the following two questions based on **one** of the titles below.

(a) Kingsley Amis: *Lucky Jim*

As part of your course, your teacher has asked you for suggestions for a story to study in class. You decide to write about *Lucky Jim*. In your report, briefly outline the plot and say why you think *Lucky Jim* would be interesting for other students.

Write your **report**.

(b) John Grisham: *The Pelican Brief*

As part of your course you have chosen to write an essay with the following title.

  'Who is the most corrupt character in *The Pelican Brief*? Give reasons for your views.'

Write your **essay**.

PAPER 3   USE OF ENGLISH (1 hour)

Part 1

For questions **1–12**, read the text below and decide which answer (**A**, **B**, **C** or **D**) best fits each gap. There is an example at the beginning (**0**).

Mark your answers **on the separate answer sheet**.

Example:

0 A instruction   **B** information   **C** opinion   **D** advice

0	A	B	C	D
	—	—	—	▬

Girls and technology

If you want your daughter to succeed, buy her a toy construction set. That is the **(0)** ..... from Britain's **(1)** ..... female engineers and scientists. Marie-Noelle Barton, who heads an Engineering Council campaign to encourage girls into science and engineering, maintains that some of Britain's most successful women have had their careers **(2)** ..... by the toys they played with as children. Even girls who end **(3)** ..... nowhere near a microchip or microscope could benefit from a better **(4)** ..... of science and technology.

'It's a **(5)** ..... of giving them experience and confidence with technology so that when they are **(6)** ..... with a situation requiring some technical know-how, they feel they can handle it and don't just **(7)** ..... defeat immediately,' says Mrs Barton. 'I believe that lots of girls feel unsure of themselves when it comes **(8)** ..... technology and therefore they might be losing out on jobs because they are reluctant even to apply for them.'

Research recently carried **(9)** ..... suggests that scientific and constructional toys should be **(10)** ..... to girls from an early age, otherwise the result is 'socialisation' into stereotypically female **(11)** ..... , which may explain why relatively few girls study science and engineering at university in Britain. Only 14% of those who have gone for engineering **(12)** ..... at university this year are women, although this figure does represent an improvement on the 7% recorded some years ago.

1 **A** foremost   **B** uppermost   **C** predominant   **D** surpassing

2 **A** styled   **B** shaped   **C** built   **D** modelled

3 **A** in   **B** by   **C** on   **D** up

4 **A** hold   **B** grasp   **C** insight   **D** realisation

5 **A** matter   **B** situation   **C** state   **D** cause

6 **A** approached   **B** encountered   **C** presented   **D** offered

7 **A** admit   **B** allow   **C** receive   **D** permit

8 **A** for   **B** to   **C** from   **D** with

9 **A** off   **B** through   **C** forward   **D** out

10 **A** accessible   **B** feasible   **C** reachable   **D** obtainable

11 **A** characters   **B** parts   **C** states   **D** roles

12 **A** options   **B** alternatives   **C** selections   **D** preferences

Part 2

For questions **13–27**, read the text below and think of the word which best fits each gap. Use only **one** word in each gap. There is an example at the beginning **(0)**.

Write your answers **IN CAPITAL LETTERS on the separate answer sheet.**

Example: | **0** | W | I | T | H | | | | | | | | | | | | | | |

Weather in Antarctica

The most extreme weather conditions experienced in Antarctica are associated **(0)** ..... blizzards. These are simply strong winds with falling snow **(13)** ..... , more commonly, snow that is picked up and pushed along the ground by the wind. Blizzards may last for days at **(14)** ..... time, and in some cases it can be almost impossible for people to see. It is not unusual **(15)** ..... objects only about a metre or **(16)** ..... away to become unrecognisable. Scientists doing research in the area **(17)** ..... then confined to their tents or caravans. We think of blizzards **(18)** ..... extremely cold, while in fact temperatures in the Antarctic are usually higher than normal **(19)** ..... a blizzard. Major blizzards of several days in length occur more frequently in some locations than in others. **(20)** ..... may be eight or ten such blizzards in any particular place **(21)** ..... an annual basis. They often cause considerable damage, so that any scientific buildings or equipment constructed in this region must be specially made to give as **(22)** ..... protection as possible.

If the weather is fine, visibility in Antarctica is usually excellent because of the clear air and the absence of dust and smoke. **(23)** ..... this means is that people often greatly underestimate the distance of objects and features of the landscape. Also, very large features **(24)** ..... as mountains may appear to be above the horizon, or even upside **(25)** ..... . These 'mirages', **(26)** ..... are just tricks played by the eyes in certain conditions, have led to explorers in the Antarctic making many errors **(27)** ..... judgement.

Part 3

For questions **28–37**, read the text below. Use the word given in capitals at the end of some of the lines to form a word that fits in the gap **in the same line**. There is an example at the beginning **(0)**.

Write your answers **IN CAPITAL LETTERS on the separate answer sheet**.

Example:

0	F	O	U	N	D	E	R										

Freud and Dreams

Sigmund Freud is regarded as the **(0)** ..... of psychoanalysis. His work   **FOUND**

has been **(28)** ..... in many areas but he is perhaps best known for   **INFLUENCE**

having drawn our **(29)** ..... to dreams, which he believed were clues to inner   **ATTEND**

conflicts. The fact that a dream is **(30)** ..... a disguised expression of what is   **ESSENTIAL**

happening in the unconscious mind means that it is difficult for the dreamer

to understand its **(31)** ..... . Freud believed that the sleeping mind resorted   **SIGNIFY**

to a whole range of unconscious wishes in forms which would prevent

the dreamer from having any **(32)** ..... of their true nature. In Freud's   **AWARE**

view, interpreting the meaning of the dream required a psychoanalyst with

an expert **(33)** ..... of how dreams disguise desires. The psychoanalyst's   **KNOW**

lack of personal **(34)** ..... in the dream would enable him to see the dream   **INVOLVE**

objectively.

According to Freud, dreams use a **(35)** ..... symbolic language quite   **MYSTERY**

different from that of waking life, but the fact is there is no hard

(36) ..... for believing that dreams really do reflect our unconscious wishes.   **EVIDENT**

Nevertheless, Freud **(37)** ..... made a major contribution to twentieth-century   **DOUBT**

thought and many useful insights into psychological processes have been

gained through his work.

Done with L4
+ L4/5
50/01/13
51/01/13

Part 4

For questions **38–42**, think of **one** word only which can be used appropriately in all three sentences. Here is an example **(0)**.

Example:

0 The committee decided to .... the money equally between the two charities.

I can't believe that John and Maggie have decided to .... up after 20 years of marriage.

To serve a watermelon you need to .... it down the centre with a sharp knife.

Example: | **0** | S | P | L | I | T | | | | | | | | | | | | |

Write **only** the missing word **IN CAPITAL LETTERS on the separate answer sheet**.

---

38 Sally's front tooth is very .... – I'm sure it'll come out soon.

Jane has lost so much weight that all her clothes are too ....

The horse got .... from the stable and started trotting towards the road.

39 The thief .... the watch into his pocket when he thought no one was looking.

Several visitors to the castle almost .... on the newly polished floor.

The speaker .... a few references to the local football team into his speech, which the audience appreciated greatly.

40 Chris arrived very early for his flight in order to be at the .... of the queue when the check-in desk opened.

My sister's got a really good .... for figures, but I'm hopeless at maths.

George has just been promoted to .... of department so he'll be even more busy from now on.

41 The restaurant .... out of fish quite early on in the evening.

The boat .... into a storm as it neared the French coast.

Mrs Benson .... the company single-handed after her husband's death.

42 This is the exact .... where the famous scene from the film was shot.

When they felt the first .... of rain, they gathered the picnic together and rushed inside.

The high .... of my trip around India was definitely the trip to Calcutta.

Part 5

For questions **43–50**, complete the second sentence so that it has a similar meaning to the first sentence, using the word given. **Do not change the word given.** You must use between **three** and **six** words, including the word given. Here is an example **(0)**.

Example:

0 Fernanda refused to wear her sister's old dress.

NOT

Fernanda said that .... her sister's old dress.

The gap can be filled with the words 'she would not wear', so you write:

Example:	**0**	SHE WOULD NOT WEAR

Write the missing words **IN CAPITAL LETTERS on the separate answer sheet**.

---

43 Mauro says he prefers to do his homework on his own.

RATHER

Mauro says that .... do his homework with other people.

44 Clara said that she had not seen the missing letter.

HAVING

Clara .... the missing letter.

45 It took Layla five minutes to find her car keys.

SPENT

Layla .... for her car keys.

46 A short meeting of the cast will take place after today's rehearsal.

BY

Today's rehearsal .... a short meeting of the cast.

47 I'll be happy to show you round the sights of my city when you come to visit me.

TAKE

It will be a .... sightseeing tour of my city when you come to visit me.

48 Rousseau painted fabulous pictures of the rainforest although he had never travelled outside Europe.

SPITE

Rousseau painted fabulous pictures of the rainforest .... travelled outside Europe.

49 It is thought that one in every five people cannot control how much they spend.

UNABLE

One in every five people is thought .... their spending under control.

50 My passport needs renewing because I'm going abroad this summer.

GET

I need .... because I'm going abroad this summer.

PAPER 4   LISTENING (approximately 40 minutes)

Part 1

You will hear three different extracts. For questions **1–6**, choose the answer (**A**, **B** or **C**) which fits best according to what you hear. There are two questions for each extract.

Extract One

You hear part of an interview with a woman who works in retail management.

1   How does the woman feel now about her first job in retailing?

   A   pleased by the way she handled the staff

   B   confident that it gave her a good start

   C   relaxed about the mistakes she made

2   What is the woman advised to do next?

   A   reflect on her skills

   B   volunteer for extra work

   C   discuss her situation with her boss

Extract Two

You overhear a woman telling a friend a story about a swan.

3   What problem did the woman have with the swan?

   A   She misunderstood its intentions.

   B   She underestimated the speed of its approach.

   C   She failed to realise the consequences of disturbing it.

4   What is the man's reaction to the story?

   A   He feels he would have handled the situation better.

   B   He is unconvinced by the woman's version of events.

   C   He fails to see quite how serious the problem was.

Extract Three

You hear part of an interview with Bruce Loader, a successful businessman who is talking about his early life.

5   Why did Bruce decide to give up the idea of studying art?

   A   He failed to gain a place at art college.

   B   He became tired of doing representational art.

   C   He was persuaded that he could not realise his ambition.

6   What was his father's reaction to Bruce's decision?

   A   He was anxious to discuss alternative employment options.

   B   He was angry that a good opportunity had been wasted.

   C   He was dismissive of the advantages of higher education.

Part 2

You will hear an explorer called Richard Livingstone talking about a trip he made in the rainforest of South America. For questions **7–14**, complete the sentences.

A Trip in the Rainforest

Richard and Matthew abandoned their boat

    because they couldn't get past a | | **7** |

They decided to walk through the jungle

    as far as the | | **8** | marked on the map.

Richard says that during the walk,

    they were always both | *and* | **9** |

The first sign of human activity that they found was a | | **10** |

In a deserted camp, they found some

    soup made from unusual | *and* | **11** |

Richard says that by the time they had reached the camp,

    they were lacking in | | **12** |

Richard says that after the meal,

    they began to feel | | **13** | about what they'd done.

Before leaving the camp,

    they left the sum of | | **14** | to thank their host.

Part 3

You will hear part of an interview with the astronaut Charles Duke, who is talking about his trip to the moon. For questions **15–20**, choose the answer (**A**, **B**, **C** or **D**) which fits best according to what you hear.

15 How did Charles feel about space travel as a boy?

    A He thought it was unlikely to happen.
    B He regarded it as more than science fiction.
    C He was fascinated by the idea of it.
    D He showed no particular interest in it.

16 What did Charles consider to be the hardest part of the training?

    A feeling trapped in the heavy spacesuit
    B endlessly practising the lunar surface landing
    C constantly being afraid of making a mistake
    D being unable to move his arms and hands

17 What was Charles's reaction when he first found out he was going to the moon?

    A He realised he had to be cautious.
    B He felt proud to be given the opportunity.
    C He tried to control his excitement.
    D He reflected on his chances of survival.

18 How did the crew feel when they had landed on the moon?

    A They felt as if they were coming home.
    B They realised they had achieved something special.
    C They were afraid of what they might find on the surface.
    D They were worried about how they would take off again.

19 What feature of the moon made the greatest impact on Charles?

    A the brightness of the sun
    B the vastness of the sky
    C the loneliness of the place
    D the absence of any stars

20 What does Charles feel was the most memorable part of his mission?

    A nearly falling into a crater
    B walking on the moon's surface
    C seeing things never seen before
    D holding a piece of the moon

Part 4

You will hear five short extracts in which people are talking about an occasion when they came into contact with a well-known celebrity.

TASK ONE

For questions **21–25**, choose from the list **A–H** what each speaker says about coming into contact with a celebrity.

A	I failed to recognise the person.	
B	I realised I had forgotten something.	Speaker 1 — 21
C	I insisted on something.	Speaker 2 — 22
D	I was upset by personal criticism.	Speaker 3 — 23
E	I had been given incorrect information.	Speaker 4 — 24
F	I was pleasantly surprised.	Speaker 5 — 25
G	I refused a request.	
H	I was amused by something.	

TASK TWO

For questions **26–30**, choose from the list **A–H** the opinion each speaker gives about the celebrity.

While you listen you must complete both tasks.

A	He/She became more agitated than necessary.	Speaker 1 — 26
B	He/She enjoyed causing trouble.	Speaker 2 — 27
C	He/She appeared totally at ease.	Speaker 3 — 28
D	He/She expected too much privacy.	Speaker 4 — 29
E	He/She seemed insincere.	Speaker 5 — 30
F	He/She wasn't able to cope with fame.	
G	He/She talked down to me.	
H	He/She eventually accepted the regulations.	

PAPER 5 SPEAKING (15 minutes)

There are two examiners. One (the interlocutor) conducts the test, providing you with the necessary materials and explaining what you have to do. The other examiner (the assessor) is introduced to you, but then takes no further part in the interaction.

Part 1 (3 minutes)

The interlocutor first asks you and your partner a few questions. The interlocutor asks candidates for some information about themselves, then widens the scope of the questions by asking about, e.g. candidates' leisure activities, studies, travel and daily life. Candidates are expected to respond to the interlocutor's questions, and listen to what their partner has to say.

Part 2 (a one-minute 'long turn' for each candidate, plus 30-second response from the second candidate)

You are each given the opportunity to talk for about a minute, and to comment briefly after your partner has spoken.

The interlocutor gives you a set of pictures and asks you to talk about them for about one minute. It is important to listen carefully to the interlocutor's instructions. The interlocutor then asks your partner a question about your pictures and your partner responds briefly.

You are then given another set of pictures to look at. Your partner talks about these pictures for about one minute. This time the interlocutor asks you a question about your partner's pictures and you respond briefly.

Part 3 (approximately 4 minutes)

In this part of the test you and your partner are asked to talk together. The interlocutor places a new set of pictures on the table between you. This stimulus provides the basis for a discussion. The interlocutor explains what you have to do.

Part 4 (approximately 4 minutes)

The interlocutor asks some further questions, which leads to a more general discussion of what you have talked about in Part 3. You may comment on your partner's answers if you wish.

Test 2

PAPER 1   READING (1 hour 15 minutes)

Part 1

You are going to read three extracts which are all concerned in some way with communication. For questions **1–6**, choose the answer (**A, B, C** or **D**) which you think fits best according to the text. Mark your answers **on the separate answer sheet**.

How useful is the term 'non-verbal expression'?

The term 'non-verbal' is commonly used to describe such communicative resources as gesture, facial movement and tone of voice. The term has long been useful in challenging the misconception that words constitute the whole of communication. However, a further assumption has sometimes seemed to follow: that 'non-verbal' expression is something unitary, independent of verbal communicating, or classifiable under some single term like 'body language'. This is to drastically simplify our actual practice. As pointed out by writers on language and social interaction, gestural and vocal actions are often integrated rather than autonomous, and verbal and non-verbal communicating usually produced in a highly coordinated fashion. Proposing a concept of 'non-verbal expression' has led to an unfounded generalisation about this supposedly distinct subject: that it is the medium for expressing emotions and relations rather than conscious thought or ideas, for example. Even if this were true, the fact remains that the resources covered by the term 'non-verbal' are diverse and complex in the extreme. It can only be misleading to bunch them together as a distinctive communicative mode.

1   The writer supports the view that non-verbal expression

   A   is more complex than verbal expression.
   B   is a separate field of study from verbal expression.
   C   is commonly used in conjunction with verbal expression.
   D   is able to communicate more information than verbal expression.

2   The writer suggests that we should

   A   recognise the differences between verbal and non-verbal expression.
   B   be aware of the many aspects of non-verbal expression.
   C   do further research into non-verbal expression.
   D   accept the limitations of non-verbal expression.

Public speaking

Last year I started work with a new company. Unfortunately, in my new role I was required to speak in public, at conferences. The thought filled me with dread, because I was sure my voice was boring. Also, I wouldn't know what to say. Anyway, when the time came I tried not to panic, and went back to first principles: I made a plan, first deciding my key message. This gave me a structure, and was the first step to dispelling my nerves.

Then I found a voice coach who taught me how to relax and breathe properly. Suddenly there was power behind my voice and I found I was in control. It was like going to a vocal gym. Instead of gabbling my sentences, I slowed down and took time to enjoy the words.

I lacked the confidence at first to speak without a script, but I learnt not to write everything down to the last word – the audience switched off when I did that. A friend gave me the tip of memorising the first few sentences, then I could make eye contact with the people I was speaking to – engage with them.

3   In this article the writer's aim is to show that

    A   public speaking need not be anything to worry about.
    B   there is always something new for a speaker to learn.
    C   it is important for a speaker to have an outgoing personality.
    D   success in public speaking depends on the quality of the speaker's memory.

4   The writer says he trained in how to speak at conferences by

    A   studying articles written by well-known public speakers.
    B   attending a course on how to give effective presentations.
    C   getting help with the physical aspects of public speaking.
    D   following colleagues' advice on ways of keeping the audience's attention.

Iowa State University: Business and Technical Communication

Essay Assignment

This assignment asks you to write an essay suitable for publication in a professional journal or newsletter. You will identify an issue that's interesting to teachers and/or workplace professionals in business and technical communication and then pose a question you want to explore about that issue. Your essay will be an argument for a clearly stated position and should be presented in a logical, understandable, and engaging manner. Your essay should be targeted to a particular journal, which means that you need to read enough articles and essays in that journal to identify their general features.

Consider the following questions:

- What are the conventions of essays in the journal or newsletter you are targeting?
- What is the question you are addressing?
- What is the argument you are making?

Cover Memo

When you submit your essay, please include a cover sheet in which you identify the features of essay conventions that you consciously employed to make the essay appropriate for the intended journal or newsletter. This is the meta-cognitive element – you knowing not only what you've done but why you did it. Please indicate the journal or newsletter to which you plan to submit your revised essay.

5   What are students expected to do in their assignment?

   A   put forward an original idea about a subject
   B   provide support for a particular point of view on a topic
   C   present an argument against an existing essay or article
   D   offer a solution to an unresolved issue in a particular field

6   Along with their essay, students are asked to provide a note which

   A   indicates the reason for their choice of topic.
   B   identifies the background texts they have read.
   C   justifies their choice of intended journal or newsletter.
   D   specifies the essay-writing characteristics used in their assignment.

Part 2

You are going to read a newspaper article about chocolate cake. Six paragraphs have been removed from the article. Choose from the paragraphs **A–G** the one which fits each gap (**7–12**). There is one extra paragraph which you do not need to use. Mark your answers **on the separate answer sheet**.

CHOCOLATE CAKE WARS

It's the most imitated cake in the world. But who created the original Sacher torte, asks Chandos Elletson?

Vienna is heaven for cake lovers. After seeing the city's sights, there is nothing better to do than sit in a coffee house and gorge on delicious cakes. These great cakes, or *tortes*, are part of Austrian folklore, and the recipes for them are closely-guarded secrets. They were invented by brilliant and creative young chefs back in the mists of time and some have even been the subject of court cases between rival confectioners. Now, inevitably, the top Viennese cakes are even available over the internet.

7	B

The date was 1832. In a royal palace outside Vienna, the Prince had sent an edict to the kitchen for a new dessert to be created in honour of some influential guests, and was anticipating something special. The head chef was ill and the order ended up with a 16-year-old pastry apprentice named Franz Sacher.

8	F

What the chef thought when he returned is unknown, but Sacher kept his recipe a secret and named the cake after himself. He went on to found his own famous hotel and café. Today, hundreds of thousands of hungry customers, most of them tourists, come each year to eat the same cake, baked to its original recipe.

9	D A

Demel, founded in 1793, was one such business. Demel himself, who was baker and confectioner for the Emperor's palace, claimed that Sacher worked for him and that their Sacher torte was the true original. A court of law decided otherwise, and only Sacher may call the cake original. The Demel Sacher torte, as it is now known, differs minutely from the Sacher, but both cakes are made with secret blends of home-made chocolate.

10	G

One contender is the Imperial Hotel in Vienna, whose Imperial torte is also sold online, and has a myth and a chef to go with it. This time it is 1873, and Emperor Franz Josef is about to inaugurate the Imperial and Royal Court Hotel. Junior cook Xavier Loibner wishes he could bake a cake for his Emperor like all the magnificent creations donated by the monarchy's top chefs.

11	E

Judging by the date, the milk chocolate would also have been a first. According to *Chocolate: The Definitive Guide*, milk chocolate was not invented until 1875, when a Swiss confectioner mixed chocolate with the condensed milk made by his friend Henri Nestlé. Whatever the origin of the story, it is said that the Emperor noticed the unusually-shaped cake. He tried it, went back for more, and so the legend of the Imperial torte was born.

Now Loibner's recipe, a secret in keeping with Viennese tradition, has recently been rediscovered and, deep in the recesses of the hotel, a dedicated production kitchen churns out thousands of these delicate cakes for dispatch all over the world.

12	A C

So the chocolate cake wars are set to continue well into the twenty-first century. Only time will tell who wins the next round of the battle. In the meantime there is plenty of opportunity to test the market.

A However, a number of rivals strongly contended that their own version of the famous cake was actually the original. As a result, a chocolate cake war raged in Vienna's coffee houses for many years.

B The most famous and most imitated of all Viennese cakes is the Sacher torte. Its recipe is still secret despite a version being available in every coffee shop you care to visit. It was invented in the days when chocolate was a luxury, available only to the very rich.

C However, Vienna's stranglehold on the internet chocolate cake market is now under threat from Paris. A well-known French chocolatier has recently joined the battle by designing a 'traveller's chocolate cake' that will be sold from his website.

D Sacher, too, manufactures its own chocolates and keeps the recipes secret, with very good reason. They once employed a foreign trainee chef who spent his time photographing everything. On his return to his home country he opened a café selling the 'original' Sacher torte.

E So he creeps into the kitchen and works through the night. By early next morning he has invented a rectangular chocolate cake made up of layers of hazelnut waffles, filled with chocolate cream, encased in marzipan and topped with milk chocolate icing. The hotel insists that this was the earliest four-sided cake to be made.

F He took his chance and in his boss's absence created a chocolate cake of such complexity that all who consumed it were stunned. His torte was a light chocolate sponge split in two halves and soaked in apricot jam before being topped with a chocolate icing. It was served with whipped cream, as it still is today.

G Now Demel have designed a new chocolate cake, called the Demel torte, for their website, firing another salvo in the chocolate cake war. And these two are not alone in the battle. They have been joined by two new rivals.

Part 3

You are going to read a newspaper article about art. For questions **13–19**, choose the answer (**A, B, C** or **D**) which you think fits best according to the text. Mark your answers **on the separate answer sheet**.

Fake art meets real money

Christophe Petyt has turned the production of exact copies of masterpieces by the world's most famous painters into big business.

Christophe Petyt is sitting in a Paris café, listing the adornments of his private art collection: several Van Goghs, and a comprehensive selection of the better Impressionists. 'I can,' he says quietly, 'really get to know any painting I like, and so can you.' Half an hour later I am sitting in his office with Degas' *The Jockeys* on my lap. If fine art looks good in a gallery, believe me, it feels even better in your hands. Petyt is the world's leading dealer in fake masterpieces, a man whose activities provoke both admiration and exasperation in the higher levels of the art world. Name the painting and for as little as £1,000 he will deliver you a copy so well executed that even the original artist might have been taken in.

Petyt's company employs over eighty painters, each steeped in the style of a particular artist or school. 'We choose them very carefully,' he says. 'They're usually people with very good technique but not much creativity, who are unlikely to make it as artists in their own right. But they love the great works and have real insight into what's gone into them.' Every work is individually commissioned, using new canvases and traditional oil paints, before being artificially aged by a variety of simple but ingenious techniques.

The notional value of the original is not the determining factor, however, when it comes to setting the retail value of Petyt's paintings. This is actually linked to the amount of effort and expertise that has gone into producing the copy. An obscure miniature may therefore cost much more than a bigger, better-known painting by a grand master. The Degas I'm holding looks as though it came off the artist's easel yesterday. Before being sold it has to be aged, and this, so to speak, is the real 'art' of the copy. A few minutes in a hot oven can put years on a canvas, black tea apparently stains it beautifully and new frames can be buried underground, then sprayed with acid.

The view when Petyt started out was that very little of this could be legal. He was pursued through the French courts by museums and by descendants of the artists, with several major French art dealers cheering from the sidelines. This concern was perhaps understandable in a country that has been rocked by numerous art fraud scandals. 'The establishment was suspicious of us,' huffs Petyt, 'but for the wrong reasons, I think. Some people want to keep all the best art for themselves.' He won the case and as the law now stands, the works and signatures of any artist who has been dead for seventy years can be freely copied. The main proviso is that the copy cannot be passed off to dealers as the real thing. To prevent this, every new painting is indelibly marked on the back of the canvas, and as an additional precaution a tiny hidden piece of gold leaf is worked into the paint.

Until he started the business ten years ago, Petyt, a former business-school student, barely knew one artist from another. Then one particular painting by Van Gogh caught his eye. At $10 million, it was well beyond his reach so he came up with the idea of getting an art-student friend to paint him a copy. In an old frame it looked absolutely wonderful, and Petyt began to wonder what market there might be for it. He picked up a coffee-table book of well-known paintings, earmarked a random selection of works and got his friend to knock them off. 'Within a few months I had about twenty good copies,' he says, 'so I organised an exhibition. In two weeks we'd sold the lot, and got commissions for sixty more.' It became clear that a huge and lucrative market existed for faux art.

Petyt's paintings are exhibited away from the traditional art centres – in places with lavish houses in need of equally impressive works of art. Although their owners include rock stars, fashion designers and top businesspeople, they either cannot afford or more likely simply cannot obtain great works of art. Petyt is understandably reluctant to name any of his clients, but says that sometimes even the owner of the original will occasionally commission a copy. 'The best paintings are so valuable,' he explains, 'that it's risky to have them at home and the costs of security and insurance are huge. So some collectors keep the original in a bank vault and hang our copy.'

Is it art? Petyt draws a parallel: 'Take music, for example. Does Celine Dion compose her own tunes – write her own lyrics? She's interpreting someone else's work, but she's still an artist. Classical musicians often try to produce a sound as close as possible to what they think the composer intended. Nobody's suggesting they're anything but artists. With us, maybe, it's the same.'

13 In the first paragraph, the writer indicates that he shares

    A Petyt's enjoyment of the work of a range of painters.

    B the art world's suspicious attitude towards Petyt's activities.

    C the general inability to distinguish copies from real paintings.

    D Petyt's desire to appreciate great works of art at close quarters.

14 What do we learn about the painters employed by Petyt?

    A They have been specially trained in the techniques of forgery.

    B They were chosen because of the quality of their original work.

    C They have to be versatile in terms of the range of styles they reproduce.

    D They make copies of those paintings which customers specifically request.

15 The price of one of Petyt's paintings tends to depend on

    A the status of the original artist.

    B the time and skill needed to create it.

    C the degree to which it has to be artificially aged.

    D the extent to which the copy truly replicates the original.

16 How does Petyt feel about the attempts to prove that his activities were illegal?

    A He suspects that they were not driven by public-spirited motives.

    B He accepts that they were useful in helping to establish his integrity.

    C He regrets that they gained the support of other art dealers in France.

    D He respects the right of the real artists' families to protect their interests.

17 As a result of the court case he won, Petyt

    A no longer reproduces fake signatures on paintings he sells.

    B has been able to copy the work of more contemporary artists.

    C is obliged to make sure his products can be identified as copies.

    D has agreed not to market his products through certain channels.

18 What do we learn about the way Petyt selected the paintings that would appear in his exhibition?

    A They needed to be ones that could be reproduced quickly.

    B It was not something that he put a great deal of thought into.

    C They had to be pictures that would appeal to the buying public.

    D He did some research into the work of artists he'd always admired.

19 What is implied about the majority of Petyt's customers?

    A They have little genuine interest in contemporary art.

    B They regard works of art as a lifestyle accessory.

    C They may buy the paintings purely as a form of financial investment.

    D They are wealthy enough to buy the original works of art if they wanted.

Part 4

You are going to read an article about leisure clothes. For questions **20–34**, choose from the sections (**A–E**). The sections may be chosen more than once.

Mark your answers **on the separate answer sheet**.

Note: When more than one answer is required, these may be given **in any order**.

Which section mentions the following?

a creation by one company that was copied by others	**20**	C
a company which decided against entering particular sporting markets	**21**	b
new clothes on the market which are attracting older customers	**22**	A
the way a company promoted itself in its early days	**23**	B C
an advantage that the current materials have over those used in the past	**24**	C
the fact that the marine clothing market is not as large as one might expect	**25**	D

a company's products being popular in unexpected markets	**26**	A	**27**	E
a company which successfully expanded its range of outdoor wear	**28**	A		
the fact that sporting clothes have become an essential part of the general clothing industry	**29**	E	**30**	B
a company which opted not to compete in the fashion market	**31**	B	**32**	D
resistance to a change in approach	**33**	B		
the kind of information that companies provide for potential customers	**34**	C		

OFFSHORE VESTMENTS

Initially designed for yachtsmen, marine clothing then unwittingly took the male fashion scene by storm.
Now this modern leisurewear is becoming increasingly popular. Keith Wheatley reports.

A

When American rap star M.C. Hammer appeared in a video draped in a baggy, high-tech Helly Hansen sailing jacket, he started a trend in nightclub fashion. The singer was more likely to have stepped from a limousine than a racing yacht (Helly Hansens were worn by the crews in the Whitbread Round the World Race) but the nautical origin of the clothes did not deter the fans. Across the US, sales began to soar – but in unlikely urban retail outlets rather than marine sales centres. Suddenly male fashion was all at sea. 'There's an element of fashion, especially with active role models, like British solo yachtsman Pete Goss,' says Sarah Woodhead, editor of the trade fashion magazine *Menswear*. 'But this marine-look, high-tech clothing thing has moved from a trend to a staple in the male clothing industry, and that's true right across Europe. It's also bringing in a new, more mature, fashion customer.'

B

Brand names that were once synonymous with yachts and epic voyages are now cropping up in every High Street. Musto, probably the biggest company in the sector, was founded some 30 years ago by Keith Musto, winner of a dinghy silver medal at the 1964 Olympic Games. The first sailing clothes were born out of Musto's frustration with the inadequate clothing then available. Now the company makes clothes worth £40 million a year. 'We wanted to branch out – away from just sailing gear, which is a smaller business than most people think,' explains Musto's son, Nigel, now marketing director. 'We discounted the fashion route as too dangerous commercially for us. Keeping people warm and dry is what we're good at.' Skiing and mountaineering were ruled out as clothes markets, either because they were too well covered by competitors, or were too small for market growth. But clothing for country pursuits was judged ripe for a vigorous commercial attack. That was over a decade ago and Musto gear now dominates the British equestrian market, from riding trousers to fleece zip-up jackets. 'The biggest barrier we faced was that it is an ultra-traditionalist market, where two factors dominated,' says Nigel Musto. 'Firstly, the belief that there was nothing better than the traditional materials simply because they had been used in the family for generations. Secondly, that the older the design of the garment was, the more style points it scored.'

C

The key to penetrating the country clothes market was to be the superior performance of modern fabrics: the fact that they are 'breathable' as well as waterproof. The basic principles of breathable fabrics have been known for two decades, and were first developed by an American company, Gore. Gore-Tex is the best known of the breathables and still the most widely used by most manufacturers. Some companies have come up with their own variants but in each case the basic technology remains the same. The manufacturers rejoice in providing pages of diagrams and acres of text which describe in minute detail exactly how each variation on the basic principle works. 'I think this is a key point in its appeal, actually,' says Sarah Woodhead. 'Customers can buy this stuff the way they would a stereo or a car.'

D

'If you'd asked me two years ago whether this surge of interest in high-tech clothing was likely, I'd have laughed,' says Helly Hansen's UK managing director, John Leaver. 'But as a society, we've become brand-besotted, so when kids decide that they want a certain look, they have an instinct for the most powerful brand in that area.' Although Leaver stresses that the company does not deliberately design clothing for the fashion conscious, he is clearly delighted with the additional sales arising from his company's strategic crossover into the mainstream marketplace. Predictably, Helly Hansen is now stocked by major department stores in their trendy leisurewear sections. 'It's provided a growth to our business that would never have been possible from a very restricted marine market,' says Leaver.

E

In 1963 Henri Strzelecki founded his company, Henri Lloyd, and the business is now one of the world's top three in the sector. From the outset, Strzelecki knew the value of publicity and did his utmost to make sure that yachting celebrities such as Sir Francis Chichester were always dressed in his products. Early on, therefore, Henri Lloyd had a secure place in a highly specialised business. Then, in the mid-1980s, huge orders suddenly started pouring in from Italy, hitherto a profitable but very small part of the sailing market. Unknown to the Strzelecki family, a large group of young people in Milan had adopted a fashionable 'uniform' which included a Henri Lloyd jacket, as worn by Sir Francis Chichester, in a distinctive blue with a red, quilted lining. The look spread across Italy, and in the Henri Lloyd factory just outside Manchester, in the north of England, machinists struggled to keep pace with demand.

PAPER 2   WRITING (1 hour 30 minutes)

Part 1

You **must** answer this question. Write your answer in **180–220** words in an appropriate style.

---

1   You are studying at an international college in Ireland. You are a member of the College Film Club, which wants to attract new members. You decide to write an article for the college magazine advertising the club. Other club members have given you ideas on what to include.

Read the information from the college Film Club website together with notes you made on the other members' ideas. Then, **using the information appropriately**, write an article for the college magazine outlining the club's activities and encouraging other students to join.

FILM CLUB

Members' ideas for article:

• mention previous speakers
• describe plans for next year
• say great way to make new friends

Now write your **article** for the college magazine, as outlined above. You should use your own words as far as possible.

Part 2

Choose **one** of the following writing tasks. Your answer should follow exactly the instructions given. Write approximately **220–260** words.

2   You see the following announcement in an international magazine.

> ### New TV show – *Hall of Fame*
>
> We are planning a series of documentary programmes on famous people who have made a positive contribution to history.
>
> Who would you nominate from your country?
>
> Write a proposal nominating ONE person from your country, and explaining why this person is important to the history of your country.

Write your **proposal**.

3   An Australian friend is writing a book about traditional festivals and customs around the world. She has asked you to write a contribution to this book, giving her details about *one* festival in your country.

Your contribution should explain the origins of the festival, describe what happens at the festival and say why you think it is still important today.

Write your **contribution** to the book.

4   You see this announcement on the noticeboard of the international college where you are studying.

> ## MAGAZINES AND NEWSPAPERS IN THE COLLEGE LIBRARY
>
> In the library we would like to offer a wider range of reading material to students studying different languages. Please write a report for the library staff recommending **one** newspaper **or** magazine that somebody learning your language would find interesting and helpful. Your report should briefly describe the newspaper or magazine and explain what somebody studying your language could learn about the culture of your country from reading it.

Write your **report**.

5   Answer **one** of the following two questions based on **one** of the titles below.

(a) Kingsley Amis: *Lucky Jim*

You've been asked to write a review of *Lucky Jim* for your college magazine. In your review, explain which character you found most likeable and why, and say whether you would recommend *Lucky Jim* to other students.

Write your **review**.

(b) John Grisham: *The Pelican Brief*

Your teacher has asked you to write an essay on *The Pelican Brief*. In your essay, briefly outline the plot, explain why it is called *The Pelican Brief* and say whether or not you enjoyed the story.

Write your **essay**.

PAPER 3   USE OF ENGLISH (1 hour)

Part 1

For questions **1–12**, read the text below and decide which answer (**A**, **B**, **C** or **D**) best fits each gap. There is an example at the beginning (**0**).

Mark your answers **on the separate answer sheet**.

Example:

0 A inhabited   **B** lived   **C** dwelled   **D** resided

0	A	B	C	D
	▬	—	—	—

The changing earth

Although the earth was formed about 4,500 million years ago, human beings have **(0)** ..... it for less than half a million years. Within this time, population has increased hugely and people have had a vast **(1)** ..... upon the earth. They have long been able to **(2)** ..... the forces of nature to use. Now, with modern technology, they have the power to alter the balance of life on earth.

Reports back from the first astronauts helped dispel the dangerous **(3)** ..... that the world had no boundaries and had limitless resources. **(4)** ..... , ecologists have shown that all forms of life on earth are interconnected, so it **(5)** ..... that all human activity has an effect on the natural environment.

In recent years, people have been putting the environment under stress. As a result, certain **(6)** ..... materials such as timber, water and minerals are beginning to **(7)** ..... short. Pollution and the **(8)** ..... of waste are already critical issues, and the **(9)** ..... of the environment is fast becoming the most pressing problem **(10)** ..... us all. The way we respond to the challenge will have a profound effect on the earth and its life support **(11)** ..... .

However, despite all these threats there are **(12)** ..... signs. Over the past few decades, the growth in population has been more than matched by food production, indicating that we should be able to feed ourselves for some time yet.

---

1 **A** imprint   **B** indication   **C** impression   **D** impact

2 **A** put   **B** make   **C** place   **D** stand

3 **A** judgement   **B** notion   **C** reflection   **D** concept

4 **A** However   **B** Likewise   **C** Moreover   **D** Otherwise

5 **A** results   **B** follows   **C** complies   **D** develops

6 **A** raw   **B** coarse   **C** crude   **D** rough

7 **A** turn   **B** come   **C** go   **D** run

8 **A** disposal   **B** displacement   **C** dismissal   **D** disposition

9 **A** state   **B** situation   **C** case   **D** circumstance

10 **A** encountering   **B** opposing   **C** meeting   **D** confronting

11 **A** projects   **B** systems   **C** methods   **D** routines

12 **A** stimulating   **B** welcoming   **C** satisfying   **D** reassuring

Part 2

For questions **13–27**, read the text below and think of the word which best fits each gap. Use only **one** word in each gap. There is an example at the beginning **(0)**.

Write your answers **IN CAPITAL LETTERS on the separate answer sheet**.

Example: | **0** | | *O* | R | | | | | | | | | | | | | | | | | | |

Early photography

In the early days of photography, a stand **(0)** ..... some other firm support for the camera was essential. This was because photographic materials were **(13)** ..... insensitive to light that a typical exposure lasted several seconds. The camera **(14)** ..... have to be held still for this time in order to obtain a sharp picture. The subjects also had to be still if their images **(15)** ..... to register properly on the film. Some early street scenes include blurred, transparent, ghostlike images of people **(16)** ..... wandered past while the scene was in the process of **(17)** ..... photographed.

Studio portraits from the late 1800s show people posed rigidly, often leaning against furniture, **(18)** ..... helped them to remain motionless. **(19)** ..... it was important to keep the head still, a support was often provided **(20)** ..... the neck. Bright studio lights, sometimes produced by **(21)** ..... fire to a strip of magnesium or a small pile of magnesium powder, helped **(22)** ..... reducing the required exposure time. These burned with an intensely blue flame that gave the necessary amount of light, **(23)** ..... the smoke was unpleasant and **(24)** ..... was also a risk of fire.

The problems associated **(25)** ..... long exposure were overcome by the introduction of faster, more sensitive photographic plates, and later, roll films. The development of smaller cameras led **(26)** ..... photography becoming a popular hobby. Nowadays, digital cameras have further revolutionised photography, enabling even the **(27)** ..... inexperienced of photographers to produce professional-looking pictures.

Part 3

For questions **28–37**, read the text below. Use the word given in capitals at the end of some of the lines to form a word that fits in the gap **in the same line**. There is an example at the beginning **(0)**.

Write your answers **IN CAPITAL LETTERS on the separate answer sheet**.

Example:

0	F	L	I	G	H	T													

The Media Commentator

A live broadcast of any public event, such as a space **(0)** ..... or sporting	**FLY**
occasion, is almost **(28)** ..... accompanied by the thoughts of a	**VARIABLE**
commentator. This may be on television, along with the relevant pictures,	
or **(29)** ..... on radio. The technique involved differs between the two media,	**ALTERNATE**
with radio broadcasters needing to be more explicit and **(30)** ..... because	**DESCRIBE**
of the **(31)** ..... of visual information. TV commentators do not need to paint a	**ABSENT**
picture for their audience; instead their various **(32)** ..... should add to the	**OBSERVE**
images that are already there. There will sometimes be silences and pauses	
in TV commentary, although these are becoming increasingly rare. Both types	
of commentator should try to be informative, but should avoid sounding **(33)**	**OPINION**
In sports commentary, **(34)** ..... and impartiality to both sides is vital, but	**FAIR**
spontaneity and **(35)** ..... are valued by those watching or listening. Sports	**ENTHUSE**
commentators usually broadcast live in an essentially unscripted way,	
although they may refer to previously prepared materials such as sports	
statistics. Because of the **(36)** ..... nature of live events, thorough	**PREDICT**
preparation in advance is vital. The internet has helped enormously with	
this aspect of the job. Anyone interested in becoming a commentator	
should have excellent organisational skills, the willingness to work	
(37) ..... hours and a strong voice.	**REGULAR**

Done with L4 + L4/5 50 ~~28~~/01/13
31/01/13

Part 4

For questions **38–42**, think of **one** word only which can be used appropriately in all three sentences. Here is an example **(0)**.

Example:

0 The committee decided to .... the money equally between the two charities.

I can't believe that John and Maggie have decided to .... up after 20 years of marriage.

To serve a watermelon you need to .... it down the centre with a sharp knife.

Example:

0	S	P	L	I	T												

Write **only** the missing word **IN CAPITAL LETTERS on the separate answer sheet**.

---

38 Nikki already had a .... idea of how she wanted her career to develop.

It soon became .... that Paula would not be able to finish the race.

The area in front of the fire exit should be kept .... at all times.

39 It's hard to .... how tall buildings are when you see them from the air.

I have been asked to .... a song-writing competition.

It's a mistake to .... people by appearances alone.

40 'I've got to go now, but I'll try to .... up with you later in the park,' said Jake.

The organisers agreed to .... the costs of clearing up after the pop concert.

The company has failed to .... its targets for the second consecutive year.

41 'We've achieved a great deal in a short .... of time,' said the company director.

Mandy liked most things about her friend's new home but thought that the dining table took up far too much ....

'I've arranged a car parking .... for you,' said the administrator.

42 My neighbour is 96 but is still able to walk without the .... of a stick.

The electronic whiteboard is a wonderful new learning .... for use in the classroom.

Flights carrying .... donated by charity organisations are now arriving in the areas affected by drought every day.

Part 5

For questions **43–50**, complete the second sentence so that it has a similar meaning to the first sentence, using the word given. **Do not change the word given**. You must use between **three** and **six** words, including the word given. Here is an example **(0)**.

Example:

0 Fernanda refused to wear her sister's old dress.

NOT

Fernanda said that .... her sister's old dress.

The gap can be filled with the words 'she would not wear', so you write:

Example: | **0** | SHE WOULD NOT WEAR

Write the missing words **IN CAPITAL LETTERS on the separate answer sheet**.

---

43 We didn't stay long at the party because it was very noisy.

SO

If .... noise, we might have stayed longer at the party.

44 The number of people applying for university grants fell last year.

FALL

There .... number of people applying for university grants last year.

45 Mr Conrad's son is becoming quite well known as an artist.

NAME

Mr Conrad's son is making .... himself as an artist.

46 Would you mind helping me carry this heavy box to the car?

GRATEFUL

This box is really heavy so I'd .... help me carry it to the car.

47 'Excuse me madam, but is this your bag?' the policeman asked.

BELONG

'Excuse me madam, but ....?' the policeman asked.

48 By the time we got to the sale, every book had been sold.

SINGLE

By the time we got to the sale, there .... book left.

49 Rosa found it very difficult to persuade her boss to give her a pay rise.

GREAT

Rosa had .... her boss to give her a pay rise.

50 The man claimed that he had been nowhere near the factory at the time of the break-in.

TO

The man claimed not .... near the factory at the time of the break-in.

PAPER 4   LISTENING (approximately 40 minutes)

Part 1

You will hear three different extracts. For questions **1–6**, choose the answer (**A**, **B** or **C**) which fits best according to what you hear. There are two questions for each extract.

Extract One

You overhear two friends, John and Diane, discussing holiday plans.

1   John thinks Diane's indecision about the holiday is

    A   unreasonable in view of her financial position.

    B   surprising since her holiday is well overdue.

    C   understandable given how much money is involved.

2   How does Diane feel about the prospect of a break from work?

    A   nervous that her boss will regret promoting her

    B   worried that staff will take advantage of her absence

    C   doubtful whether she can clear her backlog of work in time

Extract Two

You overhear two friends discussing a new film.

3   Why has the film been refused a certificate allowing it to be shown to children?

    A   The soundtrack makes it too frightening in places.

    B   The plot is too psychologically complex.

    C   The opening images are too violent.

4   The friends agree that the original story on which the film is based

    A   is written in a rather unusual style.

    B   gives a convincing portrayal of a historical character.

    C   manages to keep the reader in suspense until the end.

Extract Three

You hear an interview with the architect Ingrid Chapman, who is talking about an office building she has recently designed.

5   What does Ingrid think is the best feature of the new building?

    A   the amount of light that comes in

    B   the space she has created for staff interaction

    C   the way each floor has its own facilities

6   What does she suggest companies with outdated office buildings should do?

    A   employ her to design a more modern building

    B   ask staff what kind of workplace they would like

    C   use imagination to improve aspects of the offices

Part 2

You will hear a guide taking a group of visitors around a museum. For questions **7–14**, complete the sentences.

Museum Tour

This museum houses objects collected by the

| | 7 | based in the city.
|---|---|

It has one of the country's best galleries containing

| | 8 | exhibits.
|---|---|

The museum's displays of

| *and* | 9 | are closed to visitors at present.
|---|---|

The section called

| | 10 | is popular with young people.
|---|---|

The picture galleries contain works on various themes by

	11

The museum's

| | 12 | needs modernising.
|---|---|

The guide uses the word

| | 13 | to describe the Rutland Dinosaur's effect on people.
|---|---|

Polystyrene was used to reconstruct most of the Rutland Dinosaur's

	14

Part 3

You will hear part of a radio interview in which Harry and Jennifer, two members of an after-work adult drama class, are asked about their reasons for attending the class. For questions **15–20**, choose the answer (**A**, **B**, **C** or **D**) which fits best according to what you hear.

---

15   How does Jennifer feel about working with strangers in the class?

   A   resigned to the need for it
   B   doubtful about the value of it
   C   relaxed in her attitude towards it
   D   excited at the thought of it

16   According to Harry, the improvisation sessions

   A   require some careful preparation.
   B   enable him to use his imagination.
   C   allow him to show his acting talent.
   D   encourage him to relate to the group.

17   What does Jennifer say about improvisation?

   A   It is important not to make a mistake.
   B   It is necessary to be aware of the timing.
   C   You should be familiar with the character you invent.
   D   You need to be completely involved in the activity.

18   In Jennifer's opinion, playing written parts will

   A   be less challenging than improvisation.
   B   include research into previous performances.
   C   involve guidance from an expert.
   D   lead to competition for parts.

19   Jennifer says that the drama classes have taught her how to

   A   improve her interaction with people.
   B   manage groups of people.
   C   develop her natural acting skills.
   D   be satisfied with minor achievements.

20   Harry was annoyed because the newcomer to the group

   A   interrupted the class by arriving late.
   B   was reluctant to participate.
   C   seemed unaware of the mood of the group.
   D   wasted the tea break with pointless questions.

Part 4

You will hear five short extracts in which British people are talking about living abroad.

TASK ONE

For questions **21–25**, choose from the list **A–H** each speaker's present occupation.

TASK TWO

For questions **26–30**, choose from the list **A–H** the main advantage each speaker mentions about living where they do.

While you listen you must complete both tasks.

A	business person	
B	pensioner	
C	doctor	
D	farmer	
E	diplomat	
F	student	
G	engineer	
H	architect	

Speaker 1	B	21
Speaker 2	H	22
Speaker 3	D	23
Speaker 4	A	24
Speaker 5		25

A	a beautiful language	
B	friendly people	
C	luxury accommodation	
D	a good climate	
E	interesting challenges	
F	varied sports	
G	a high salary	
H	excellent food	

Speaker 1	F	26
Speaker 2		27
Speaker 3		28
Speaker 4	C	29
Speaker 5		30

Visual materials for the Speaking test

Why are the flags being used?

What effect might they have on people who see them?

What do the wheels enable people to do?
How important may they be?

How effective might these suggestions be in improving health care?
Which two suggestions would benefit the local community most?

C3

Why do children enjoy games like these?

What might children learn from playing them?

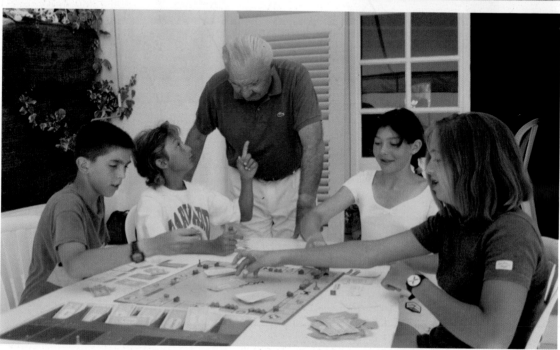

What feelings are being expressed?
What might have made the people feel like this?

How great might the demand be for these improvements?
Which would be the most, and which the least, effective in attracting more passengers?

How practical is it to store things in these ways?
How easy might it be for people to find what they are looking for?

What kind of customer might they attract?

What might be the advantage of shopping in these places?

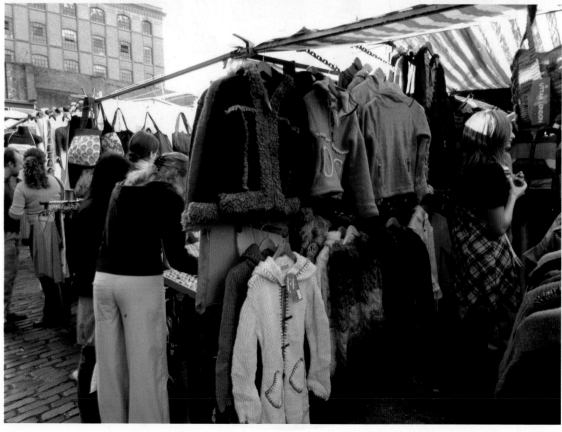

How can the weather conditions affect people's lives?
Which two kinds of weather conditions could have the most harmful effects?

What aspects of the past do the photographs show?
How might the people be feeling as they look back on the past?

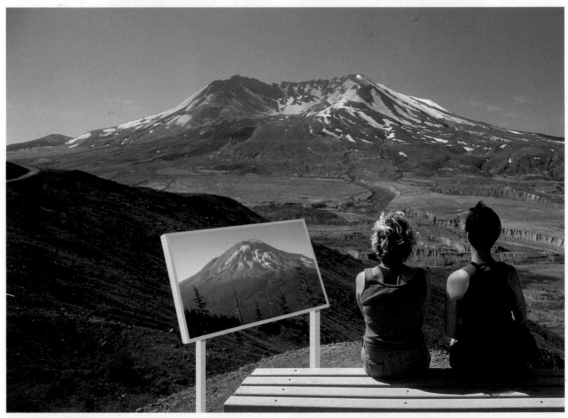

What might have caused these events?
How could they have been prevented?

How might these activities help people escape from the pressures of everyday life?
Which two would have the most lasting benefit?

PAPER 5 SPEAKING (15 minutes)

There are two examiners. One (the interlocutor) conducts the test, providing you with the necessary materials and explaining what you have to do. The other examiner (the assessor) is introduced to you, but then takes no further part in the interaction.

Part 1 (3 minutes)

The interlocutor first asks you and your partner a few questions. The interlocutor asks candidates for some information about themselves, then widens the scope of the questions by asking about, e.g. candidates' leisure activities, studies, travel and daily life. Candidates are expected to respond to the interlocutor's questions, and listen to what their partner has to say.

Part 2 (a one-minute long turn for each candidate, plus 30-second response from the second candidate)

You are each given the opportunity to talk for about a minute, and to comment briefly after your partner has spoken.

The interlocutor gives you a set of pictures and asks you to talk about them for about one minute. It is important to listen carefully to the interlocutor's instructions. The interlocutor then asks your partner a question about your pictures and your partner responds briefly.

You are then given another set of pictures to look at. Your partner talks about these pictures for about one minute. This time the interlocutor asks you a question about your partner's pictures and you respond briefly.

Part 3 (approximately 4 minutes)

In this part of the test you and your partner are asked to talk together. The interlocutor places a new set of pictures on the table between you. This stimulus provides the basis for a discussion.

The interlocutor explains what you have to do.

Part 4 (approximately 4 minutes)

The interlocutor asks some further questions, which leads to a more general discussion of what you have talked about in Part 3. You may comment on your partner's answers if you wish.

Test 3

Part 1

You are going to read three extracts which are all concerned in some way with dance. For questions **1–6**, choose the answer (**A**, **B**, **C** or **D**) which you think fits best according to the text. Mark your answers **on the separate answer sheet**.

A choreographer's diary

May saw the premiere of my first full-length narrative ballet – *The Ballet Shoes* – for the London Children's Ballet. I have to say, I was wondering if it was going to come off or not. In the studio the week before, I could see nothing exciting – no action. The dancing was coming along okay but the children's acting seemed stiff and contrived. Well, that's one lesson I've learned – don't worry about children performing. Or at least, not until they reach a shy/awkward adolescence where self-criticism overrides any fun. No, as soon as this lot set foot on the stage, the dance floor might as well have been a trampoline. They were well and truly stage-struck, jumping and whirling around like crazy.

Thanks to the efforts of too-many-people-to-mention, the premiere went according to plan. I wasn't really able to watch it objectively that night but when I came back to see the last show – the seventh performance in four days, I was actually smiling along with most of the audience. I have to admit to having watery eyes and after twenty-odd Sundays of losing my voice, all was forgotten and I was very proud of 'my children'!

1   What does the writer suggest about the dancers in *The Ballet Shoes*?

   A   They were better actors than dancers.
   B   They were too young to be self-conscious.
   C   They lacked sufficient enthusiasm for ballet.
   D   They learnt ballet techniques amazingly quickly.

2   When watching the last performance of *The Ballet Shoes*, the writer

   A   believed her hard work had been worthwhile.
   B   was surprised by the reaction of the audience.
   C   thought that the show had got better each night.
   D   felt relieved that it was all over.

Opening Night

On Tuesday I went to the opening night of choreographer Ella Winter's new dance show. The work was produced in collaboration with a linguist, a landscape designer, a heart surgeon and an architect. The score, by Antonio Prandini, samples Italian folk songs and their lyrics. There is a minimalist set – white boxes – incorporating a video installation. And there are Winter's eight dancers. The dance involves mechanical-looking repeated-action sequences and a running montage of mimed laughs, whistles, hissing breaths, and twists of the feet. At times, the dancers enact the lyrics of the songs – there are brief fragments of duet – but long sections are difficult to understand or merely banal. Many hands, on this occasion, had not made light work.

At times, I found myself musing on Winter's collaborators. According to Winter, they had given her and her dancers different objectives, and each had brought a method of expression which had not been available to the dancers before. No doubt, but it's hard to view the result, as Winter claims, as something unique in the sphere of contemporary dance. I've been an admiring spectator of Winter as both dancer and choreographer for over 30 years now, but I felt subtly defeated by the show. For me, it seemed a private conversation with a like-minded few. You had to be wearing very strong contemporary-dance goggles to make anything of it.

3   What does the writer say about the show in the first paragraph?

    A   It is unclear which part each collaborator had contributed to.
    B   Too many people were involved in the project.
    C   The dance movements didn't match the music.
    D   The dancers had very different views on the roles they should play.

4   What was the writer's opinion of the show?

    A   It had appeal for a very specific audience.
    B   Each dancer had a unique form of expression.
    C   The choreographer's long experience was evident.
    D   It was very different from other forms of contemporary dance.

A system to notate dance

For at least five centuries attempts have been made to devise a system of notation to record the sequence of movements in dances. Scholars believe that the ancient Egyptians made use of hieroglyphs to do this and that the Romans employed a method of notation for formal gestures. However, the earliest known attempt, recorded in two manuscripts preserved in the Municipal Archives of Cervera, Spain, dates from the second half of the fifteenth century. Since that time, many other systems have been devised. Some were published and achieved a measure of popularity for a while, but almost all, until the present day, fell eventually into disuse.

It is significant that music notation, which opened the way for development in the art of music as we know it today, was first conceived in its modern form in the eleventh century, but was not established as a uniform system till the beginning of the eighteenth. Dance notation got off to a much later start and has undergone a long succession of false attempts. That so many unsuccessful beginnings were made is not surprising. Dance is more complex than music because it exists in space as well as in time and because the body itself is capable of so many simultaneous modes of action. Consequently, the problems of formulating a movement notation that can be easily written and read are numerous.

5   What do we learn about systems to notate movement from the first paragraph?

    A Researchers have different views about how the systems were used.
    B The evidence regarding the use of early systems is unreliable.
    C One system was used in more countries than the others.
    D Some systems have been in use longer than others.

6   Why does the writer make comparisons between music notation and dance notation?

    A to explain why music notation took so long to develop
    B to emphasise the difficulties involved in dance notation
    C to illustrate the similarities between the two forms of notation
    D to describe how notation has affected the development of both art forms

Part 2

You are going to read an extract from a newspaper article about coral reefs. Six paragraphs have been removed from the extract. Choose from the paragraphs **A–G** the one which fits each gap (**7–12**). There is one extra paragraph which you do not need to use. Mark your answers **on the separate answer sheet**.

Reef Encounter

Tropical fish look very colourful to our eyes, but is that how they look to each other? Our reporter Penny Gosh met the man who may have the answer.

If you're snorkelling around a coral reef, you'll see the local marine life in all its carnival colours. But the show clearly isn't just a tourist attraction. For the fish that live on the reef, it's more a matter of life and death. As with any other creature, the survival of a fish species depends on two things – food supplies and breeding success.

7

Seeing a coral reef in all its glory, you can't help feeling that fish have completely failed to solve this dilemma. The picture, however, only comes into focus when you take the fish's-eye view. For fish, according to Justin Marshall from the Vision, Touch and Hearing Research Centre at the University of Queensland in Brisbane, see things differently.

8

This means that the carnival looks quite different to the marine life itself. To help him discover exactly how different it looks, Marshall has designed a unique underwater 'spectrophotometer', which analyses the colours of things objectively in terms of their physical reflection. He is also measuring the light available in different micro-habitats.

9

The general shift towards the blue end of the spectrum in underwater light explains why most nocturnal reef fish, such as the soldierfish, squirrelfish and big-eyes, are mainly red in colour. According to Marshall, some reef fish might see red, in which case they could capitalise on the colour blindness of others and use red markings for private communication. But in most cases, red species are surprisingly inconspicuous.

10

As any snorkeller will know, lots of reef fish display the sort of colour combinations that suggest camouflage is the last thing on the fish's mind. The bright blues and yellows that are most common, however, are only conspicuous at a certain range. They fade to grey at a distance, because the colours are so close together that they merge.

11

Wider colour bands will be visible much farther away, of course, but still the fish's-eye view is different from ours. Most recently, Marshall has discovered that fish may see hardly any contrast between the blue of many species, such as tropical angelfish, and the colour of the water around a tranquil reef. More surprisingly, says Marshall, a fish with blue and yellow stripes can be just as well camouflaged, as even this distinct pattern will merge into some backgrounds. When the fish are all together in a shoal, it's hard for a predator to spot where one individual starts and another ends. It's what Marshall calls 'the zebra effect'. If Marshall is correct, then a fish with bold blue and yellow markings can either advertise or hide itself by simply adjusting its behaviour.

12

In other words, one set of colours can send out very different signals depending on the setting. To complicate things further, most reef fish can vary their colours, whilst it is common for species to change colour from night to day or as they grow older. Colours may even change with a fish's mood – whether it's fighting or fleeing from predators.

A   Together with information about the visual sensitivity of individual fish species and their behaviour, this equipment enables him to begin seeing things as fish do. And it is starting to reveal how the showy and the shy can make use of the same bright colours.

B   This is because our visual system is a primate one, he says. It's very good at seeing yellows and reds versus greens. However, 30 metres below sea level there is no red light. So fish tend to see blues and ultraviolets well – and to be less sensitive to reds and yellows.

C   The striking bands of colour seem to shout 'come and get me' to a potential mate when displayed against a plain background or close up. But put them up against a background of solid contrasting colours and they work on the same principle as the disruptive camouflage used for concealment of military equipment.

D   The trouble is that eating and not being eaten both need stealth. Therefore, it is helpful for a fish to blend into the background. To attract a mate, on the other hand, requires a certain flamboyance.

E   If this means that fish really can't see the difference, then it looks to him as though they have only two types of receptors for colour. This is a controversial claim, as others have argued that fish have four types of colour receptor.

F   During the day, such fish hide in reef crevices. Once there, they may look obvious to human eyes, but to other fish, they blend into the dark background.

G   Even in fish which sport fine stripes, such as parrotfish and wrasse, the different shades are distinct for only one metre and certainly no more than five. Beyond this, they too blend into the general sea colour around the reef.

Part 3

You are going to read a newspaper article. For questions **13–19**, choose the answer (**A, B, C** or **D**) which you think fits best according to the text. Mark your answers **on the separate answer sheet**.

Lights, camera, action man

Travel journalist Richard Madden reports on his first trip with a camera crew.

It was books that first captured my imagination about faraway places. TV travelogues always seemed the poor relation to the classic written accounts, although of course the pictures were rather better. And then there was the issue of authenticity. All those pretentious theatrical types dying of thirst in the desert, as if we didn't realise there was a camera crew on hand to cater for their every need. These days programme-makers know that the audience is more sophisticated and the presence of the camera is acknowledged. But can a journey with filming equipment ever be anything other than a cleverly constructed fiction?

I recently got the chance to find out, when I was asked to present two one-hour programmes for an adventure travel series. The project was the brainchild of the production company Trans-Atlantic Films, which wanted the series presented by writers and adventurers, as well as TV professionals. My sole qualification was as a journalist specialising in 'adventure' travel. However, I was thought to have 'on-screen' potential.

The first programme was filmed in Costa Rica. Within 24 hours of my arrival, I realised that this was going to be very different from my usual 'one man and his laptop' expeditions. For a start, there were five of us – director, cameraman, sound recordist, producer and presenter. And then there was the small matter of £100,000 worth of equipment. I soon realised that the director, Peter Macpherson, was a vastly experienced adventure film-maker. In his case, the term 'adventure' meant precisely that. 'Made a film with X,' he would say (normally a famous mountaineer or skier), before describing a death-defying sequence at the top of a glacier in Alaska or hang-gliding off the Angel Falls in Venezuela. Invariably, these reminiscences would end with the words: 'Had a great deal of respect for X. Dead now, sadly . . .'

Part of the brief for the series was to put the presenter in unusual situations and see how he or she coped. One such sequence was the night we spent in the rainforest canopy near the Rincón de la Vieja National Park in Guanacaste province. I don't have a head for heights and would make a poor rock-climber, so my distress is real enough as the camera catches me dangling on a rope some 30 metres up, well short of the canopy platform.

Ironically, it was the presence of the camera, looking down on me from above, that gave me the impetus for the final push to the top. By this time, I'd learnt how 'sequences' were cut together and realised that one last effort was required. I had to struggle to stay coherent while the camera swooped within a few millimetres of my face for my reaction. In the end, it was a magical experience, heightened all the more by the sounds of the forest – a family of howler monkeys in a nearby tree, amplified through the sound recordist's headphones.

Learning how to establish a rapport with the camera is vital and it took me a while to think of it as a friend rather than a judge and jury. The most intimidating moments were when Peter strolled up to me, saying that the light would only be right for another 10 minutes, and that he needed a 'link' from one sequence to another. The brief was simple. It needed to be 30 seconds long, sum up my feelings, be informative, well-structured and, most important of all, riveting to watch. 'Ready to go in about five minutes?' he would say breezily.

I soon discovered that the effect of the camera on what was going on around us was far less intrusive than I had imagined. After a first flurry of curiosity, people usually lost interest and let us get on with our job. We were also flexible enough to be spontaneous. Our trip coincided with an 80 per cent solar eclipse, a rare event anywhere in the world. We were in a village called Santa Elena and captured the whole event on camera. The carnival atmosphere was infectious and made a welcome addition to our shooting schedule.

13 One thing the writer used to dislike about travel programmes on TV was

    A the repetitive nature of many of them.
    B the dull images that they frequently contained.
    C their lack of respect for the intelligence of the viewers.
    D their tendency to copy the style of famous written accounts.

14 What reason is given for the writer becoming involved in making TV travel programmes?

    A other people's belief that he might be suited to appearing on them
    B his own desire to discover whether it was possible to make good ones
    C his own belief that it was natural for him to move from journalism to TV
    D a shortage of writers and adventurers willing to take part in them

15 Shortly after arriving in Costa Rica, the writer became aware that

    A the director had a reputation that was undeserved.
    B he would probably dislike working as part of a team rather than alone.
    C he would probably get on well with the director personally.
    D his role in the filming would be likely to involve real danger.

16 The writer uses the sequence filmed in the National Park as an example of

    A something he had been worried about before any filming started.
    B the sort of challenge that presenters were intended to face in the series.
    C something he was expected to be unable to deal with.
    D the technical difficulties involved in making films in certain places.

17 What does the writer say about the last part of the sequence in the National Park?

    A It taught him a lot about the technical aspects of film-making.
    B He was encouraged to complete it when he looked up at the camera.
    C It changed his whole attitude towards doing dangerous things.
    D He was unable to say anything that made sense at this time.

18 In paragraph six the writer says that he found it particularly difficult to

    A understand what was required of him for a 'link'.
    B change things he was going to do at very short notice.
    C accept certain advice given to him about presenting a film.
    D meet certain demands the director made on him.

19 What does the writer use the experience in Santa Elena as an example of?

    A something they filmed although they had not planned to
    B the friendly way in which they were treated by the local people
    C something they did purely for their own enjoyment
    D the kind of thing that viewers like to see in travel films

Done with L4
07/02/14

Part 4

You are going to read an article about mazes. For questions **20–34**, choose from the sections (**A–E**). The sections may be chosen more than once.

Mark your answers **on the separate answer sheet**.

Which section mentions the following?

a maze whose layout can be varied	**20**	C
the fact that making economies can result in a maze not being accessible at all times	**21**	E
a maze which is no longer unique	**22**	D
the positive advantages of mazes which are not open to everyone	**23**	C
an improvement to a particular design	**24**	B
the fact that when planting a maze it is easy to exceed the original estimate	**25**	C
the suitability of a particular country for cultivating mazes	**26**	B
the fact that mazes are pointless in terms of a practical function	**27**	A
a maze which reflects the owner's interests	**28**	B
a method of finding your way round one maze	**29**	D
a body which looks down on mazes	**30**	E
the amount of maintenance a maze requires	**31**	B
the appeal of mazes to a certain type of mind	**32**	C
the fact that mazes do not have a clear path to the centre	**33**	C
the fact that people have not been put off by disapproval	**34**	E

Mazes

There are few rules to having your own maze, although getting the design right is one of them.
Then sit back and wait for a few years. Rupert Wright loses himself in the thick of it all.

A

There is something enduringly eccentric about mazes. They serve no useful purpose, except perhaps to entertain guests you don't want to see for the afternoon. But the English are mad about them. The Royal Horticultural Society rather frowns on mazes, regarding them as a bit of an oddity, but this has not deterred a nation's gardeners. The second largest maze in the world is at Longleat House in Wiltshire; the largest turf maze is at Saffron Walden, Essex. Adrian Fisher, the world's leading maze designer, is English. His firm designs and builds more than 250 a year worldwide, many for private individuals.

B

One of Adrian Fisher's recent creations is for banker Lord Sandberg in the grounds of his estate. The design of the maze celebrates both his passion for cricket and his career in banking. 'I thought it would be fun,' says Lord Sandberg. 'My great-great-grandchildren will be able to run around it and think of me. The only snag is that all the yew trees we planted last year have died, so I am back to square one.' In principle, assuming the plants are not diseased, growing a hedge in a temperate climate such as England's is straightforward. It requires less work and care than a lawn. The hedge will need clipping just once a year. After ten years it will be a decent enough size to get lost in.

C

One Microsoft director is planning to build a maze in the garden of his house in the south of France. Another Microsoft employee is starting work on an elaborate 10-metre-wide decorative pavement maze. Perhaps there is something particularly attractive about mazes to software engineers; we have all experienced that moment when we are stuck in a piece of software and cannot get out. 'One of the beauties of a private maze is that you can have all sorts of things that would not be practical in a public maze, where there are health and safety concerns,' says Adrian Fisher. 'In one maze, I designed a series of angled mirrors disguised in some overhanging arches in order to disorientate people,' he says. 'In another, a three-metre section of hedge rotates on a turntable to change the puzzle design in a few seconds. There is also a

cunningly designed wooden bench with hedges behind. Hit the right button and they all roll backwards to reveal a hidden passage to one side.'

D

Mazes have a long and distinguished history. King Minos of Crete instructed Daedalus to build a labyrinth 3,500 years ago. The difference between a labyrinth and a maze is that a labyrinth follows one track towards the middle; a maze is full of trickery, dead ends and wrong turns. The most famous maze in the world is probably the Hampton Court maze in England. There are more than 15 copies of the maze throughout the world. The original was built in 1690. It can be easily penetrated by keeping one's left hand on the wall. This works because the hedge that surrounds the centre is continuously connected to the perimeter hedge. Later, mathematically minded maze makers, such as the Earl of Stanhope, solved this problem by creating 'islands', or gaps in the hedges. Using the Hampton Court technique at Stanhope's best example at Chevening would be pointless. If you keep your left hand on the hedge at Chevening, you end up being spat out again at the beginning.

E

There is something inherently furtive and secretive about a maze. Adrian Fisher is designing a private maze for an individual who plans to give summer parties. Round the first corner guests will be served drinks, then left to their own devices to find their way to the centre, where a band will be playing. Once the party is assembled, various decorative maze gates will be opened. The cost of building a maze is a bit like building a garden: it all depends on size and the number of plants, and if you are not careful, the budget continues to grow. The cost of building hardcore paths adds considerably to the cost, but many people don't bother, preferring just to use the mazes when the conditions underfoot are good. One drawback is the amount of time one has to wait for the hedge to grow. Half the fun of having a maze is watching it grow and knowing that it will be enjoyed for years. Most people turn to an experienced designer. Some, though, decide to design their own mazes, although there are pitfalls: one man who pursued this path watched with satisfaction as the hedge grew beautifully, only to discover that the maze did not work.

PAPER 2   WRITING (1 hour 30 minutes)

Part 1

You **must** answer this question. Write your answer in **180–220** words in an appropriate style.

---

1   You are the secretary of the student committee at an international college. The Principal is planning an Open Day and has asked you for your comments on a programme of events.

Read the email from the Principal below. Then, **using the information appropriately**, write a report making recommendations and justifying your choices.

From: principal@cxx.ac.uk
Subject: Open Day
The Open Day must provide publicity for the college – and be interesting!
What do you think of these ideas:
–   opening speech – me (history of college) OR former student (memories of college life)?
–   canteen open to the public OR international dishes cooked by students?
–   do you think it would be a good idea to give demonstration lessons?
–   could you suggest a suitable student to show visitors round the college?

Now write your **report** for the Principal, as outlined above. You should use your own words as far as possible.

Part 2

Choose **one** of the following writing tasks. Your answer should follow exactly the instructions given. Write approximately **220–260** words.

2   You read the following announcement in a travel magazine.

> ### TOURISM – IS IT GOOD OR BAD FOR YOUR REGION?
>
> Do you think there should be more or less tourism in your region?
> What benefits does the tourist industry bring to your region?
> What would be the disadvantages of increased tourism?
>
> Write and tell us your views. We will publish the most interesting articles.

Write your **article**.

3   You see this announcement in an international education magazine.

> ### BEST TEACHER COMPETITION
>
> *Everyone remembers their best teacher.*
>
> We want you to nominate one of your teachers for our Best Teacher award. Send us your competition entry, telling us about the best teacher that you have ever had.
>
> Your entry should:
> - describe what the teacher taught you
> - explain how this teacher has influenced your life
> - tell us why this teacher deserves to win the award.

Write your **competition entry**.

4   An international student magazine has asked its readers to send in a review of **two** different websites that are useful for students. Write a review for the magazine in which you compare **two** different websites, including the following points:
- what kind of information each website contains
- how easy each website is to use
- why these sites are useful for students.

Write your **review**.

5   Answer **one** of the following two questions based on **one** of the titles below.
(a) Kingsley Amis: *Lucky Jim*

You see this notice in an international film magazine.

> We would like you, our readers, to send in an article recommending a story you think would make a good film and giving reasons for your opinions.

You decide to write an article recommending *Lucky Jim*.

Write your **article**.

(b) John Grisham: *The Pelican Brief*

As part of your course, your teacher has asked you to write an essay on the importance of politics to the storyline of *The Pelican Brief*. Outline what part politics plays in the story and say whether you think these events could happen in real life.

Write your **essay**.

PAPER 3   USE OF ENGLISH (1 hour)

Part 1

For questions **1–12**, read the text below and decide which answer (**A**, **B**, **C** or **D**) best fits each gap. There is an example at the beginning (**0**).

Mark your answers **on the separate answer sheet**.

Example:

0 A primary   **B** dominant   **C** leading   **D** principal

0	A	B	C	D
	—	—	**▬**	—

Dinosaur discoveries

In the late 1930s, a group of **(0)** ..... American scientists seeking dinosaur fossils made some noteworthy finds. Although one of their expeditions discovered no fossils, it nonetheless **(1)** ..... to be important in terms of the information about dinosaurs it provided. During that historic expedition, which took place along the **(2)** ..... of the Paluxy river in Texas, something extraordinary was revealed: a dinosaur track, clearly **(3)** ..... in the rock. These dinosaur footprints **(4)** ..... their preservation to the salts and mud that covered them and then hardened into rock, before **(5)** ..... to light 100 million years later. Tracks like these are **(6)** ..... to experts. There have been great gaps in scientists' understanding of dinosaur **(7)** ..... , and so such footprints are useful since they provide direct **(8)** ..... of how dinosaurs actually moved. Scientists have used these and other footprints to determine how quickly different species walked, concluding that many kinds of dinosaur must have travelled in **(9)** ..... .

(10) ..... , the tracks of four-legged dinosaurs seem to **(11)** ..... that, in spite of being reptiles, these creatures must have moved in a very similar way to living mammals, such as elephants – a pattern of movement **(12)** ..... from that of most contemporary reptiles, such as crocodiles. This leads to an interesting question. Might existing mammals have more to teach us about the extinct reptiles that once walked the earth?

1 **A** turned   **B** arose   **C** proved   **D** occurred

2 **A** verges   **B** borders   **C** coasts   **D** banks

3 **A** blatant   **B** substantial   **C** distinguishable   **D** ostensible

4 **A** owe   **B** derive   **C** result   **D** thank

5 **A** coming   **B** bringing   **C** appearing   **D** surfacing

6 **A** unique   **B** invaluable   **C** costly   **D** rare

7 **A** action   **B** manners   **C** behaviour   **D** customs

8 **A** basis   **B** support   **C** source   **D** evidence

9 **A** sets   **B** herds   **C** masses   **D** bunches

10 **A** Appropriately **B** Characteristically **C** Interestingly **D** Alternatively

11 **A** point   **B** specify   **C** express   **D** indicate

12 **A** separate   **B** unconnected   **C** detached   **D** distinct

Part 2

For questions **13–27**, read the text below and think of the word which best fits each gap. Use only **one** word in each gap. There is an example at the beginning **(0)**.

Write your answers **IN CAPITAL LETTERS on the separate answer sheet**.

Example: | 0 | | O | U | R | | | | | | | | | | | | | | | | |

The Best Books

Are there 1,000 books that all of us should read sometime in **(0)** ..... lives? Throughout this year, we will be recommending a collection of books that, when taken **(13)** ..... a whole, will form a library of 1,000 titles that will inspire and satisfy **(14)** ..... kind of reader imaginable. Book lists appear from time to time, often arousing controversy **(15)** ..... being too elitist or too populist. But our list is the result of consultations with bookbuyers and booksellers, people **(16)** ..... know and love books.

Currently, there are well **(17)** ..... a million books in print. Add **(18)** ..... these another 100,000 books published each year and the choice for readers becomes bewildering, **(19)** ..... certain books, both classics and contemporary works, stand out. While our list doesn't identify classics **(20)** ..... the traditional sense, many of the works included **(21)** ..... considered to be classic books. The list aims to make the reader aware of **(22)** ..... is available that is stimulating, rewarding and inspiring. **(23)** ..... else does one learn about a good read other **(24)** ..... by enthusiastic recommendation?

This month we are highlighting fifty books from the area of business and reference. These fifty titles represent the perfect business and reference library for your needs, **(25)** ..... personal or professional. Our selection will help you to expand and enhance **(26)** ..... understanding of today's fast-changing world of business.

Look out for next month's fifty choices, **(27)** ..... will take you a step nearer completion of your 1,000-book library.

Part 3

For questions **28–37**, read the text below. Use the word given in capitals at the end of some of the lines to form a word that fits in the gap **in the same line**. There is an example at the beginning **(0)**.

Write your answers **IN CAPITAL LETTERS on the separate answer sheet**.

Example:

0	I	N	D	E	P	E	N	D	E	N	T						

Volunteer Project in Lesotho

Lesotho is a small **(0)** ..... nation in the middle of southern Africa.	**DEPEND**
The **(28)** ..... of Lesotho lies more than 1,000 metres above sea level.	**KING**
With its wild **(29)** ..... landscapes, it is a paradise for nature lovers and	**SPOIL**
outdoor **(30)** ..... , and also offers the opportunity for visitors to gain	**ENTHUSIASM**
(31) ..... experience of African culture. This is particularly true in the rural	**PRACTICE**
areas, where the distinctive and **(32)** ..... traditions of the country are still	**COLOUR**
very much alive.	

Volunteers are now needed for two related projects for a community-	
based organisation in the Maletsunyane gorge, a remote and	
spectacular region in the highlands of Lesotho. One project will	
involve improving the **(33)** ..... track used by both visitors and locals to	**HAZARD**
reach the base of a waterfall in the gorge. For the second project,	
volunteers are needed to **(34)** ..... a biodiversity survey of the region.	**TAKE**
(35) ..... , much of this area is suffering from overgrazing, hunting and	**FORTUNE**
other activities which threaten the **(36)** ..... of the land.	**SUSTAIN**

Volunteers will be accommodated in shared rooms. There is a communal	
kitchen, and also a chance to experience the local restaurants. Special	
dietary **(37)** ..... can be provided for if advance notice is given.	**REQUIRE**

Part 4

For questions **38–42**, think of **one** word only which can be used appropriately in all three sentences. Here is an example **(0)**.

Example:

0 The committee decided to .... the money equally between the two charities.

I can't believe that John and Maggie have decided to .... up after 20 years of marriage.

To serve a watermelon you need to .... it down the centre with a sharp knife.

Example: | **0** | | S | P | L | I | T | | | | | | | | | | | | | | |

Write **only** the missing word **IN CAPITAL LETTERS on the separate answer sheet**.

---

38 The new law means that the tax system will .... in a different way from now on.

Before you .... this machinery, make sure you are wearing the appropriate safety gear.

The surgeon decided not to .... as he felt that the patient's condition would improve without surgery.

39 'I think this would be a good .... at which to take a break,' said the tour guide.

Everyone agreed with Janine's .... that the accounts could have been falsified.

The students felt discouraged because what they were doing didn't seem to have any ....

40 Stella bought the .... for her new living-room curtains in the market and made them up herself.

Jake is going to Italy to get .... for his new historical novel, which will be set in Ancient Rome.

A waterproof .... such as plastic or glass should be used to cover the top of the box.

41 The group .... a new album last month.

The engineer .... the safety catch carefully and then started the machine.

Last year the factory .... five per cent more toxic fumes into the atmosphere.

42 I think that your brother will .... an excellent doctor when he qualifies.

I am afraid I can't .... the meeting on Saturday because I'm busy.

What do you .... of the new manager in the production department?

Part 5

For questions **43–50**, complete the second sentence so that it has a similar meaning to the first sentence, using the word given. **Do not change the word given**. You must use between **three** and **six** words, including the word given. Here is an example **(0)**.

Example:

0 Fernanda refused to wear her sister's old dress.

NOT

Fernanda said that .... her sister's old dress.

The gap can be filled with the words 'she would not wear', so you write:

Example:	**0**	SHE WOULD NOT WEAR

Write the missing words **IN CAPITAL LETTERS on the separate answer sheet**.

---

43 It is essential that this door is kept unlocked.

SHOULD

On no .... locked.

44 It seems unbelievable that this jewellery is almost a thousand years old when it is so well preserved.

HARD

This jewellery is in such good .... believe that it is almost a thousand years old.

45 When it comes to punctuality, Fiona really takes after her mother.

CONCERNED

As ...., Fiona really takes after her mother.

46 You have to be very patient to work as a primary school teacher these days.

DEAL

Working as a primary school teacher calls .... these days.

47 He didn't understand exactly what was wrong until he read Julie's letter.

ONLY

It .... he read Julie's letter that he understood exactly what was wrong.

48 None of the other team members supported Terry's idea.

SUPPORT

Terry's idea met with .... the other members of the team.

49 The region is rich in natural resources.

OFFER

The region has a lot .... terms of natural resources.

50 Because of its price, the book may never become a bestseller.

PREVENT

The price of the book may .... a bestseller.

PAPER 4   LISTENING (approximately 40 minutes)

Part 1

You will hear three different extracts. For questions **1–6**, choose the answer (**A, B** or **C**) which fits best according to what you hear. There are two questions for each extract.

Extract One

You hear two colleagues, Eva and Colin, talking about a problem at work.

1   What is Colin's opinion of their new boss?

   A   She fails to consult with colleagues.

   B   She is too keen to establish new working practices.

   C   She has little understanding of the organisation's history.

2   When talking about the problem, Eva is

   A   trying to suggest that it is unimportant.

   B   comparing alternative ways of solving it.

   C   encouraging Colin to take a more positive attitude to it.

Extract Two

You hear an interview with an expert who repairs antique vases.

3   What is the expert doing at the start of the interview?

   A   explaining what can ruin a restoration job

   B   comparing various methods of restoration she uses

   C   describing the difficulties of matching colours during restoration

4   How does the expert feel about leaving visible cracks in the finished vase?

   A   They should be avoided if at all possible.

   B   They are part of the vase's history and should be seen.

   C   They affect the value of the vase rather than its appearance.

Extract Three

On the radio, you hear a visitor talking to a man about the remote island where he lives.

5   The man wants a ferry service between the mainland and the island because

   A he is keen to develop tourism on the island.

   B he thinks more young people would come to live on the island.

   C he feels the island people should not be isolated from modern life.

6   The speakers have different opinions about whether

   A creating an airport would be advantageous.

   B building houses on the beach would be advisable.

   C commercial development would spoil the island's unique nature.

Part 2

You will hear a short radio report about how technology is helping archaeologists who want to learn more about some texts written over 2,000 years ago known as Roman tablets. For questions **7–14**, complete the sentences.

ROMAN TABLETS

The speaker says that an Ancient Roman 'tablet' was about as thick as a present-day

	7

At the site of an old

	8

, archaeologists discovered about 200 tablets.

Roman soldiers often used tablets when writing letters or documents of a

	9

nature.

On one tablet mentioned, the word

	10

is legible as well as

people's names.

An expert in what's called

	11

says that the project is very challenging.

Panels on the tablets were once filled with

	12

, which provided the writing surface.

Efforts to analyse the original texts using

	13

photography were unsuccessful.

New technology is also being applied to other historical texts which were written using

ink	**14**

Part 3

You will hear an interview with an architect called Lucy Collett who designs small buildings. For questions **15–20**, choose the answer (**A**, **B**, **C** or **D**) which fits best according to what you hear.

15 Lucy enjoyed building the tree-house because it

    A gave her children somewhere to play.
    B presented an interesting design problem.
    C demonstrated the type of work she does.
    D allowed her to fulfil a childhood ambition.

16 What fascinated Lucy about the historical phone boxes?

    A their international character
    B their luxurious interiors
    C their range of styles
    D the quality of their construction

17 At college, Lucy designed small buildings so that they

    A could be assembled in a shorter time.
    B would comply better with safety rules.
    C would have a wider range of uses.
    D could be built in a simpler style.

18 Lucy got the idea for a folding market stall

    A from her parents.
    B from travelling salesmen.
    C while she was at a trade fair.
    D while she was on an overseas trip.

19 What did Lucy like best about her award-winning design?

    A the shape
    B the display space
    C the decoration
    D the building material

20 The hotel phone booths which Lucy worked on were

    A developed with mobile phone users in mind.
    B designed for countries with relatively few mobile phones.
    C placed at the entrance to the hotel lobby.
    D intended to be the largest feature of the lobby.

Part 4

You will hear five short extracts in which people are talking about problems related to their work.

TASK ONE

For questions **21–25**, choose from the list **A–H** the problem each person encounters.

TASK TWO

For questions **26–30**, choose from the list **A–H** each person's current feeling.

While you listen you must complete both tasks.

A	a troublesome client	
B	poor pay and conditions	
C	a difficult colleague	
D	conflict with management	
E	a failed project	
F	excessive responsibility	
G	a lack of promotion	
H	an inefficient IT system	

Speaker 1   **21**

Speaker 2   F   **22**

Speaker 3   H   **23**

Speaker 4   E   **24**

Speaker 5   B   **25**

A	keen to bring in changes	
B	willing to accept their situation	
C	sure that things will improve	
D	reluctant to make a complaint	
E	annoyed by messages from colleagues	
F	aware of their own failings	
G	miserable in their present job	
H	unsure what to do about the problem	

Speaker 1   F   **26**

Speaker 2   C   **27**

Speaker 3   G   **28**

Speaker 4   E   **29**

Speaker 5   H   **30**

PAPER 5 SPEAKING (15 minutes)

There are two examiners. One (the interlocutor) conducts the test, providing you with the necessary materials and explaining what you have to do. The other examiner (the assessor) is introduced to you, but then takes no further part in the interaction.

Part 1 (3 minutes)

The interlocutor first asks you and your partner a few questions. The interlocutor asks candidates for some information about themselves, then widens the scope of the questions by asking about, e.g. candidates' leisure activities, studies, travel and daily life. Candidates are expected to respond to the interlocutor's questions, and listen to what their partner has to say.

Part 2 (a one-minute 'long turn' for each candidate, plus 30-second response from the second candidate)

You are each given the opportunity to talk for about a minute, and to comment briefly after your partner has spoken.

The interlocutor gives you a set of pictures and asks you to talk about them for about one minute. It is important to listen carefully to the interlocutor's instructions. The interlocutor then asks your partner a question about your pictures and your partner responds briefly.

You are then given another set of pictures to look at. Your partner talks about these pictures for about one minute. This time the interlocutor asks you a question about your partner's pictures and you respond briefly.

Part 3 (approximately 4 minutes)

In this part of the test you and your partner are asked to talk together. The interlocutor places a new set of pictures on the table between you. This stimulus provides the basis for a discussion.

The interlocutor explains what you have to do.

Part 4 (approximately 4 minutes)

The interlocutor asks some further questions, which leads to a more general discussion of what you have talked about in Part 3. You may comment on your partner's answers if you wish.

Test 4

PAPER 1 READING (1 hour 15 minutes)

Part 1

You are going to read three extracts which are all concerned in some way with people living together. For questions **1–6**, choose the answer (**A**, **B**, **C** or **D**) which you think fits best according to the text. Mark your answers **on the separate answer sheet**.

WRITING MY FAMILY MEMOIRS

One problem when writing family histories is knowing how to show people what your family is like. Recording their recollections is the best method, but this is difficult if, like my family, they communicate chiefly through shrugs and raised eyebrows. At one point I thought I had so little material I'd have to give up altogether, but then it dawned on me – my family may be an extreme case, but this is true to a certain extent of all families. Being so familiar with each other, we had learnt to read each other's facial expressions like meteorologists reading a sky.

One of my most potent teenage memories is of taking charge of some sick chickens on our family farm. I built them a special pen, and spent my spare time feeding them. When I told my dad they had all died, I realised he had known this would happen, and that he would not have let my brother, a trainee farmer, persist in such a sentimental illusion. In short, it meant that everyone had realised before I did that I'd never make a farmer. Did my brother, father or mother remember the chickens as a major turning-point, too? No: they did not remember them at all. The only person who did was my sister. She had helped me with them herself – only for me, in my self-absorption, to subsequently forget about her. I soon realised how separate we all are, and that you can only ever tell your own story.

1   In the first paragraph, what does the writer say happened during the course of his research?

   A   He learnt to understand his own family's manner of communication.
   B   He realised his family was not very different from other families.
   C   He found a way of presenting his family to the reading public.
   D   He changed his opinion of the relationships within his family.

2   What is the writer's purpose in recounting the episode about the chickens?

   A   to highlight the differences in personality between the members of his family
   B   to emphasise how attitudes to people and events can change over time
   C   to underline the need to achieve a balanced view of a past occurrence
   D   to demonstrate the subjective nature of people's memories

Living on a commune

Communes have existed since history was first recorded. I grew up on one in the late 1960s, when more than 2,000 were formed in the USA. However, I was never sure what exactly a commune was defined as: only what it was like to live on one. When I left the commune at twelve years old, I was astounded to encounter almost entirely negative views of communes from people in 'mainstream' society.

There are two main types of communes. In the 'anarchistic commune' there is an agreement to reject establishment and organizational worlds. Usually anyone is welcome, members are temporary, and there are no rules. This type of commune usually doesn't last long. For example, the Oregon Farm, a small and short-lived rural commune, emphasized individualism so much so that there were no real guidelines for living – no norms for membership, behaviour or meal times. Members were transient and there were many arguments about who got what and why, and about work. For example, the women felt it was unfair that they had all the housework and childcare responsibilities while the men worked in the fields.

The second type is the 'service commune', in which people pool resources and agree to live a certain way with a motivating philosophy. Membership is more closed, residents must commit to the commune's purpose. This type is socially organized with leaders and rules. Usually this type of commune has a sense of purpose that binds the people within the commune together toward a common goal.

3 What does the writer imply about communes in the first paragraph?

    A They are better than life in mainstream society.
    B They are generally misunderstood.
    C They are ideal places for children.
    D They are of very little value.

4 What is the main difference the writer identifies between 'anarchistic' and 'service' communes?

    A the people who join the commune
    B the division of work on the commune
    C the reason for setting up the commune
    D the areas of conflict within the commune

Interviewing Londoners

A common ingredient in all the memories which people shared with me, as they looked back and thought about how they remembered their lives in a poor district of London in the 1930s and 40s, was a real sense of loss for the time when 'we were all one'. A time when you knew all your neighbours; when you sat outside the front door of your house on a kitchen chair during long summer nights chatting and when you helped each other if you had problems, without a second thought. And yet this affection is probably the result of hindsight. When families were living in such close proximity there could have been little opportunity for peace and quiet and even less for privacy.

A striking example of how things have changed in our perception of what we might expect from our local community was seen in the response to my questions about the problems of organising childcare. Women either needed me to explain what I was talking about or they laughed: what need was there for such formalised arrangements when you were part of a large whole which looked out for one another, regardless of whether they were family, friends or simply your next-door neighbour? It wasn't an issue. If a woman worked, and many did – had to – there was always someone to keep an eye out for the kids. That's the way it worked.

5   In the first paragraph, the writer suggests that the people he interviewed

    A   were bewildered by the changes in their lives.
    B   were disillusioned by family life.
    C   were objective in their view of the past.
    D   were influenced by a sense of nostalgia.

6   What does the writer imply by saying that the women laughed?

    A   They wished that modern arrangements had been available in the 1930s.
    B   They identified with the writer's difficulties in finding childcare.
    C   They recognised that childcare was a common problem nowadays.
    D   They thought that childcare hadn't needed to be organised in the 1930s.

Test 4

Part 2

You are going to read a newspaper article about a sport. Six paragraphs have been removed from the article. Choose from the paragraphs **A–G** the one which fits each gap (**7–12**). There is one extra paragraph which you do not need to use. Mark your answers **on the separate answer sheet**.

After the Frisbee

It used to be as simple as a bit of fun in the park. Now the Frisbee is back – and this time it's serious business. Simon de Burton reports.

Until recently, the name 'Gucci' was synonymous with expensive handbags and jewellery. Now however, the company's 'G-force' slogan has taken on a whole new meaning, with the introduction of the Gucci Flying Disc, a 20-centimetre diameter circle of semi-flaccid rubber that retails at a smooth £35. This piece of flying fun has literally taken off, leaving Gucci's main stores with a waiting list of customers that grows longer by the day.

7

The difference now is that flying discs are no longer the exclusive domain of college students. Frisbee-throwing has developed into a range of serious sub-sports, from a team game called Ultimate to the unlikely-sounding disc golf, with distance, accuracy, discathon and freestyle Frisbee falling in between.

8

Assistant librarian and disc-throwing fanatic, Brian Dacourt may not quite fit in with the trend in this respect. He is, however, chair of the World Flying Disc Federation and established the first Ultimate world championships in 1986 when just six teams took part. This year there were more than 100. 'It has become a sport played predominantly by professional people,' he says. 'After graduating, they have progressed up the career ladder into powerful jobs before returning to disc sports much more seriously in their free time.'

9

The team version of Frisbee-throwing, the game of Ultimate, is currently enjoyed by around 700 serious players in the UK. Teams are made up of seven players, and the aim of the game is to score goals by passing the disc to a player standing or running inside the opposition's 'end zone'.

10

But Ultimate's rules do not seem to give rise to the dissension, fouls and gamesmanship that some, more prestigious, sports suffer from. A key Ultimate phrase is 'the spirit of the game', which refers to the sport's basic code of conduct. Even at world championship level, referees or linesmen are not needed.

11

The names of Frisbee-related sports are a little more accessible. An individual version of Frisbee-throwing known as 'disc golf' has also grown up, courtesy of financial expert Derek Robins. Robins, Chairman of the British Disc Golf Association, charges just £3 for a round at his course beside the River Avon.

12

Therefore, when players reach the spot on the course where their last throw has landed, they can choose a disc which is the most appropriate one for the next throw – in much the same way that golfers might use a driver from the tee – with the aim of 'holing out' the disc, into an iron basket held up by a chain, in the minimum number of throws.

It is all a far cry from the early days of the Frisbee in the 1870s, when William Russell Frisbie patented his Frisbie pies, in the disc-shaped tins that college students so delighted in throwing to each other, after eating the pies.

88

A In keeping with this air of gentlemanly camaraderie and enthusiastic innovation, a whole new language has evolved among the game's devotees. Words such as 'force', 'hammer', 'poach', and 'stall' are used to describe the various moves, throws and tactics which the game demands.

B Even a top-class competitor in several of these disciplines would not have to fork out much on equipment compared to other sports. However, the relative cheapness is somewhat at odds with the nature of its devotees: more and more it tends to be high-earning lawyers, stockbrokers, bankers and IT professionals who make up the core of serious players.

C Once in possession of the disc, a player is not allowed to run with it; it has to be worked up the pitch through a series of tactical passes. If it touches the ground or is intercepted, possession passes to the opposition.

D The popularity of this particular brand of disc bears testament to the fact that the fun-filled summers of the 1970s, when Frisbees in parks were a common sight, are enjoying something of a revival.

E But if all this sounds a little too energetic, and you are happy just to chuck a Frisbee to a friend in the park, you will be in good company. Old-style Frisbee fans can still count among their numbers several famous names, including a leading Hollywood movie star and a Formula One driver.

F The rules are similar to those of the famous sport from which it is derived, the obvious difference being the use of flying discs instead of balls and clubs. Players walk the course with a range of five or more special discs which have special edges and are made of denser material than an Ultimate disc, thus allowing them to fly further.

G Indeed, the sport very much reflects the lifestyles of the people who play it. It is all about working together with one's side against the opposition; competitiveness and camaraderie are of the utmost importance.

Part 3

You are going to read a newspaper article. For questions **13–19**, choose the answer (**A**, **B**, **C** or **D**) which you think fits best according to the text. Mark your answers **on the separate answer sheet**.

Travelling sensitively

A tour operator which specialises in environmentally sensitive holidays has banned the use of all cameras. Is this the future of tourism? asks Mark Hodson.

The days of the camera-toting tourist may be numbered. Insensitive travellers are being ordered to stop pointing their cameras and camcorders at reluctant local residents. Tour companies selling expensive trips to remote corners of the world, off the well-trodden path of the average tourist, have become increasingly irritated at the sight of visitors upsetting locals. Now one such operator plans to ban clients from taking any photographic equipment on holidays. Julian Matthews is the director of *Discovery Initiatives*, a company that is working hand-in-hand with other organisations to offer holidays combining high adventure with working on environmental projects. His trips are not cheap; two weeks of white-water rafting and monitoring wildlife in Canada cost several thousand pounds.

Matthews says he is providing 'holidays without guilt', insisting that *Discovery Initiatives* is not a tour operator but an environmental support company. Clients are referred to as 'participants' or 'ambassadors'. 'We see ourselves as the next step on from eco-tourism, which is merely a passive form of sensitive travel – our approach is more proactive.'

However, says Matthews, there is a price to pay. 'I am planning to introduce tours with a total ban on cameras and camcorders because of the damage they do to our relationships with local people. I have seen some horrendous things, such as a group of six tourists arriving at a remote village in the South American jungle, each with a video camera attached to their face. That sort of thing tears me up inside. Would you like somebody to come into your home and take a photo of you cooking? A camera is like a weapon; it puts up a barrier and you lose all the communication that comes through body language, which effectively means that the host communities are denied access to the so-called cross-cultural exchange.'

Matthews started organising environmental holidays after joining a scientific expedition for young people. He subsequently founded *Discovery Expeditions*, which has helped support 13 projects worldwide. With the launch of *Discovery Initiatives*, he is placing a greater emphasis on adventure and fun, omitting in the brochure all references to scientific research. But his rules of conduct are strict. 'In some parts of the world, for instance, I tell people they should wear long trousers, not shorts, and wear a tie when eating out. It may sound dictatorial, but I find one has a better experience if one is well dressed. I don't understand why people dress down when they go to other countries.'

Matthews' views reflect a growing unease among some tour companies at the increasingly cavalier behaviour of well-heeled tourists. Chris Parrott, of *Journey Latin America*, says: 'We tell our clients that indigenous people are often shy about being photographed, but we certainly don't tell them not to take a camera. If they take pictures without asking, they may find themselves having tomatoes thrown at them.' He also reports that increasing numbers of clients are taking camcorders and pointing them indiscriminately at locals. He says: 'People with camcorders tend to be more intrusive than those with cameras, but there is a payoff – the people they are filming get a tremendous thrill from seeing themselves played back on the viewfinder.'

Crispin Jones, of *Exodus*, the overland truck specialist, says: 'We don't have a policy but, should cameras cause offence, our tour leaders will make it quite clear that they cannot be used. Clients tend to do what they are told.'

Earthwatch, which pioneered the concept of proactive eco-tourism by sending paying volunteers to work on scientific projects around the world, does not ban cameras, but operates strict rules on their use. Ed Wilson, the marketing director of the company, says: 'We try to impress on people the common courtesy of getting permission before using their cameras, and one would hope that every tour operator would do the same. People have to be not only environmentally aware but also culturally aware. Some people use the camera as a barrier; it allows them to distance themselves from the reality of what they see. I would like to see tourists putting their cameras away for once, rather than trying to record everything they see.'

13 In the first paragraph we learn that *Discovery Initiatives*

    A offers trips that no other tour company offers.
    B organises trips to places where few tourists go.
    C has decided to respond to its customers' complaints.
    D has already succeeded in changing the kind of tourist it attracts.

14 Julian Matthews thinks that the function of the company is to

    A get people involved in environmental work.
    B influence the way other tour companies operate.
    C inform holidaymakers about environmental damage.
    D co-operate with foreign governments to promote eco-tourism.

15 What does Matthews say in the third paragraph about cameras and camcorders?

    A They give local people a false impression of holidaymakers.
    B They discourage holidaymakers from intruding on local people.
    C They prevent local people from learning about other societies.
    D They encourage holidaymakers to behave unpredictably.

16 What is Matthews keen for clients to realise?

    A that certain behaviour may spoil their enjoyment of a trip
    B that they may find certain local customs rather surprising
    C that it is likely that they will not be allowed in certain places
    D that the brochure does not contain all the information they need

17 Which of the following does Chris Parrott believe?

    A Tourists are unlikely to agree to travel without their cameras.
    B Local people may react angrily towards tourists who use cameras.
    C Tourists are becoming more sensitive about their use of cameras.
    D Camcorders always cause more trouble with local people than cameras.

18 Crispin Jones says that his company

    A expects its staff to prevent problems over the use of cameras.
    B seldom encounters problems regarding the use of cameras.
    C is going to decide on a firm policy regarding the use of cameras.
    D advises clients about the use of cameras before they leave.

19 Which of the following best summarises the view of *Earthwatch*?

    A Too many tour operators ignore the problems caused by cameras.
    B Most tourists realise when they have caused offence to local people.
    C There are more problems concerning the use of cameras these days.
    D Cameras enable people to be detached from places they visit.

Part 4

You are going to read an article about over-consumption. For questions **20–34**, choose from the sections (**A–D**). The sections may be chosen more than once.

Mark your answers **on the separate answer sheet**.

Which section mentions the following?

the impact on people of organisations seeking greater efficiency	20
an explanation of why happiness is always out of reach	21
the fact that people's attitudes towards certain goods have changed over time	22
data that has revealed a surprising lack of correlation	23
a lack of evidence that people today are more content than they used to be	24
the ability of the market to meet people's desire to acquire more goods	25
those aspects of life which are neglected in the pursuit of affluence	26
the feeling that many people have of being unable to escape the demands of a growth economy	27
the countries where it is accepted that people's happiness is reliant on them having ever-increasing levels of material wealth	28
the writer's acceptance that there may be something beneficial in the wide availability of certain products	29
research that shows the role of certain preconceptions in determining people's responses	30
the economic damage that would occur if people stopped aspiring to higher levels of material wealth	31
the extent to which maintaining a growth economy requires people to put important areas of their lives at risk	32
the suggestion that people are primarily motivated by the need to earn sufficient money to live on	33
the way in which business practices can manipulate people's perceptions of what they need	34

Over-consumption

Paul Wachtel asks why economic growth does not automatically lead to an increased sense of well-being.

A

In a host of different ways, the economies of the highly industrialised nations of the world have long operated on the assumption that a sense of well-being depends crucially both on the quantity of goods and services available to the population and on the rate at which that quantity is growing. It is easy to understand how such a misconception could hold sway. And yet, there is little indication that people's lives are fuller or happier than those of our parents' or grandparents' generation, who had much 'less'.

Why *is* it that growth has yielded so little in enduring satisfaction? Why do people fail to derive any pleasure from their standard of living when, in fact, they have so much more than the previous generation? To explicate fully the ironies and psychological contradictions of the emphasis on economic growth would require considerably more space than is available here, but to begin with, it must be noted that the entire dynamic of the growth-oriented economies that exist in industrialised countries absolutely *require* dissatisfaction. If people begin to be satisfied with what they have, if they cease to organise their lives around having still more, the economy is in danger of grinding to a halt.

B

The tendency to over-consume results, in part, from advertising. The very purpose of modern advertising is to generate desires; if an ad can make you feel your life is not complete without product X, it has done its job. But ads are not the only source of this phenomenon. Society as a whole is structured to lead people to define their aspirations in terms of products, and new products are constantly being brought out. Moreover, this tendency is exacerbated considerably by another set of psychological factors. A variety of studies have demonstrated that judgements about an experience are shaped very largely by a person's level of expectation. In a growth-oriented society, people's expectations are continually being raised, and so their adaptation level – the level against which they compare new experiences – keeps rising. Only what is above the new standard ever gets noticed. Satisfaction becomes like the horizon; it looks a clear and finite distance away and potentially attainable. But as you approach it, it continually recedes, and after much effort you are no closer than you were when you began.

C

People's expectations being too high is not the only reason for the ambiguous relationship between material goods and a sense of well-being. Many of the ways we gear up for growth actually *undermine* some of the more fundamental sources of satisfaction and well-being, leaving us feeling more insecure and less satisfied than we were before. A number of major studies into sources of happiness concluded that once some minimal income is attained, the amount of money people have matters little in terms of bringing happiness. In other words, above the poverty level, the relationship between income and happiness is remarkably small. What does matter, these studies indicate, are things like love, friendship, being part of a community, being committed to or part of something larger than oneself. But it is precisely these things that a way of life organised around growth and market transactions impairs. The expectations, assumptions, and arrangements by which people in the industrialised world live, lead them to sacrifice a great deal, both individually and collectively, for the sake of perpetuating the economic system.

D

Nowadays, we work too hard as we strive to be able to afford the larger and larger package that defines a standard way of life and we make our working lives less pleasant as we, societally, forget that the workers from whom we extract greater productivity are ourselves, and as more people feel the insecurity of corporate efforts to become 'lean and mean'. And all too often, people attribute all the hours of work not even to the wish to 'make it', but simply to the fact that they must 'make ends meet'. For most people in the West, there is simply the experience of having to keep up with the treadmill. Yet what figures comparing present purchasing power with those prevailing in the 1950s and 1960s (an earlier time of perceived prosperity) show, is that the definition of 'making ends meet' keeps changing. What not too long ago would have defined an upper-middle-class standard of living now feels to most people as 'just making ends meet'. The dishwasher, television set and so forth that once were signs of luxurious living are now perceived to be necessities. Perhaps this is a sign of progress and certainly there *is* something salutary about the fact that we no longer regard as luxuries such items as running water. But as the definition of necessity keeps evolving, we need to bear two things in mind: that the sense of well-being does not increase in the same way and that the earth is groaning under the strain.

PAPER 2   WRITING (1 hour 30 minutes)

Part 1

You **must** answer this question. Write your answer in **180–220** words in an appropriate style.

---

1   You are studying at an international college. Ms Johnson, the Principal, has asked you to write a proposal on library facilities at the college.

Read Ms Johnson's email below and the notes you have made. Then, **using the information appropriately**, write a proposal to her, explaining why you think the improvements are necessary and outlining how the facilities could be improved.

---

email   Page 1 of 1

From: djohnson@cax.ac.uk
Sent: 15 March 2006
Subject: Library facilities

Can you write a proposal saying what you think we
need to do to improve the library? Money is limited   *too*
so we can't do everything. Can you say which of these   *short!*
things you think are the most important: opening
hours, work space, books, videos, IT, other resources
not — or anything else you can think of.
enough
                                  old + boring   *English*
                                                     magazines?

Thanks

Sue Johnson

Now write your **proposal** for Ms Johnson, as outlined above. You should use your own words as far as possible.

Part 2

Choose **one** of the following writing tasks. Your answer should follow exactly the instructions given. Write approximately **220–260** words.

2   You see the following announcement in a telecommunications magazine:

KEEPING IN TOUCH

Are relationships with families and friends and face-to-face contact with people under threat from the increased use of modern technology such as email and mobile phones?
Does this technology help to improve real communication or should we get out and meet each other more?

Write and tell us what you think, giving reasons for your views. We will publish the most interesting articles.

Write your **article**.

3   An English-speaking friend is doing some research on public transport around the world and has asked for a contribution from you.

Write a contribution for your friend's research, explaining:

• how important public transport is in your area
• why people are willing or unwilling to use it
• what you think should be done to improve public transport in your area.

Write your **contribution**.

4   You have seen the following advertisement in an international newspaper.

ISLAND ADVENTURE

We are looking for 30 people to take part in an exciting new television programme. If you are chosen, you will all be taken to an island and left for six months with only basic supplies. Have you got the necessary skills to survive? Have you got the right personality to work in a team? Tell us why you want to participate and why you should be chosen.

Write your **letter of application**.

5   Answer **one** of the following two questions based on **one** of the titles below.

(a) Kingsley Amis: *Lucky Jim*

You have been asked to write an essay on Jim Dixon's attitude to work. In your essay, describe how Jim's attitude to work influences his actions and say whether or not you sympathise with his behaviour.

Write your **essay**.

(b) John Grisham: *The Pelican Brief*

Your college magazine has asked you to write an article on the 'bad guys' in *The Pelican Brief*. Your article should describe the role these villains play in the story and say how you think they add to the excitement of the plot.

Write your **article**.

PAPER 3   USE OF ENGLISH (1 hour)

Part 1

For questions **1–12**, read the text below and decide which answer (**A**, **B**, **C** or **D**) best fits each gap. There is an example at the beginning (**0**).

Mark your answers **on the separate answer sheet**.

Example:

0 A scenery   **B** panorama   **C** spectacle   **D** outlook

Example: | **0** | A — | B — | C — | D — |

A guidebook writer

He is five thousand metres up in the Peruvian Andes, with a view of magnificent **(0)** ..... all around. Looking down at the snow-capped mountains **(1)** ..... out below, Peter Hutchison can be **(2)** ..... for thinking that he has the best job in the world. But the **(3)** ..... required to keep it sometimes **(4)** ..... him out. Some days his head **(5)** ....., not from lack of oxygen but from the **(6)** ..... of checking rooms in fifty different hotels.

Peter is in charge of a team of writers working on a series of travel guidebooks. 'Each guidebook contains hundreds of thousands of facts,' he says. 'When I am on a research trip, I sometimes note down eighty points of **(7)** ..... in one day. **(8)** ..... to popular belief, being a travel writer is no holiday! So that others can get the most out of their trips, I have to **(9)** ..... long hours.'

After driving himself hard for a week, Peter **(10)** ..... himself by taking a few days off to **(11)** ..... his own favourite leisure activities, which include scuba-diving and jungle treks. He has an amazingly comprehensive knowledge of South America. 'I'd love to live here permanently,' he says, 'but I have to return to London to chase up the other contributors and make sure the latest book doesn't fall behind **(12)** .... It's due out in October and mustn't be late.'

1 **A** expanding   **B** spreading   **C** broadening   **D** lying

2 **A** mistaken   **B** tolerated   **C** spared   **D** forgiven

3 **A** force   **B** power   **C** effort   **D** attempt

4 **A** wears   **B** brings   **C** works   **D** bears

5 **A** turns   **B** spins   **C** winds   **D** twists

6 **A** strain   **B** affliction   **C** suffering   **D** distress

7 **A** interest   **B** attention   **C** value   **D** attraction

8 **A** Opposite   **B** Contrary   **C** Alternative   **D** Distinct

9 **A** put in   **B** take up   **C** make over   **D** get into

10 **A** celebrates   **B** delights   **C** rewards   **D** praises

11 **A** perform   **B** pursue   **C** maintain   **D** attend

12 **A** timetable   **B** programme   **C** schedule   **D** agenda

Part 2

For questions **13–27**, read the text below and think of the word which best fits each gap. Use only **one** word in each gap. There is an example at the beginning **(0)**.

Write your answers **IN CAPITAL LETTERS on the separate answer sheet.**

Example:

0	W	I	T	H	O	U	T												

The history of the cinema

In Britain, the cinema was, **(0)** ..... doubt, the most important form of public commercial entertainment of the twentieth century. Until its popularity was eclipsed in the 1950s by television, cinema enjoyed a period of some fifty years during **(13)** ..... its appeal far exceeded **(14)** ..... of sport or indeed any other commercial leisure activity.

The popularity of the cinema at that time is **(15)** ..... difficult to explain: it was accessible, glamorous and cheap. At **(16)** ..... height, between 1920 and 1950, a very small sum of money **(17)** ..... guarantee a good seat in the cinema. In the 1920s, the usual venue was a small, neighbourhood hall. The audience was drawn from the local area, and could **(18)** ..... some occasions be rather noisy. By the end of the 1930s, **(19)** ..... , the venue was more likely to be in **(20)** ..... of the larger cinemas known as 'picture palaces', which were springing up everywhere in city centres **(21)** ..... accommodate audiences of over two thousand people. **(22)** ..... these establishments, the audiences were expected to be well behaved; the performances were organised just **(23)** ..... military operations, **(24)** ..... uniformed staff on hand to control the queues and usherettes to direct seating arrangements.

These large cinemas attracted **(25)** ..... very mixed audience, although older people were less likely to be cinema-goers than adolescents. As might be expected, people in rural areas were **(26)** ..... immersed in the cinema than were people in towns, simply **(27)** ..... of the greater provision of cinemas in urban areas.

Part 3

For questions **28–37**, read the text below. Use the word given in capitals at the end of some of the lines to form a word that fits in the gap **in the same line**. There is an example at the beginning **(0)**.

Write your answers **IN CAPITAL LETTERS on the separate answer sheet**.

Example:

0	W	E	S	T	E	R	N												

How music was written down

The familiar **(0)** ..... system of notation – writing down music using symbols –   **WEST**

has taken thousands of years to develop. In ancient times, elaborate music

was in **(28)** ..... , even though it was never written down. Eventually, however,   **EXIST**

(29) ..... felt the need to record their music, and so the search began   **CIVILISE**

for a system of symbols that could **(30)** ..... denote the exact pitch of the   **RELY**

note to be sung or played, and at the same time tell the **(31)** ..... how long   **PERFORM**

that note should be held.

The ancient Greeks and Romans did this by using their alphabetical letters

in a **(32)** ..... of ways, but the slow development of notation could not keep   **VARY**

pace with **(33)** ..... complex musical developments. The 13th century saw   **INCREASE**

the introduction of colours to represent more complex note values.

With the invention of printing in the 15th century, the writing of notes was

(34) ..... to black and white and the number of lines became fixed at five.   **STANDARD**

By the middle of the 18th century, musical notation had settled down to its

modern usage.

The main **(35)** ..... to this system has been the adoption of expression marks,   **ADD**

which multiplied **(36)** ..... in the 19th century. These convey the composer's   **SIGNIFY**

intentions as regards speed, **(37)** ..... and so on, to the player   **INTENSE**

or singer.

Part 4

For questions **38–42**, think of **one** word only which can be used appropriately in all three sentences. Here is an example **(0)**.

Example:

0 The committee decided to .... the money equally between the two charities.

I can't believe that John and Maggie have decided to .... up after 20 years of marriage.

To serve a watermelon you need to .... it down the centre with a sharp knife.

Example: | **0** | S | P | L | I | T | | | | | | | | | | | | |
|---|---|---|---|---|---|---|---|---|---|---|---|---|---|---|---|---|---|

Write **only** the missing word **IN CAPITAL LETTERS on the separate answer sheet**.

---

38 Professor Nilsson is one of the leading experts in the .... of genetic research.

The company wanted to purchase the football .... so as to build a new supermarket there.

The walkers were told that they did not have permission to cross the ....

39 The company .... its awards ceremony in March last year.

John .... the ladder firmly while his father painted the window frame.

The file that was destroyed .... some extremely important information.

40 I told the builders that the wall .... rather damp when I touched it.

Dr Rowan .... that it was time for him to retire after fifteen years as chairman.

Karin .... in her bag hoping her wallet was there.

41 There is unlikely to be any .... in the weather this week.

Johann says he is really looking forward to his holiday because he needs a ....

Could you let me have some .... for the parking meter?

42 My father gave me a lift into town and .... me at the railway station.

The estate agent .... the asking price for the house in the hope of a quick sale.

Without any warning a piece of plaster suddenly .... from the ceiling.

Part 5

For questions **43–50**, complete the second sentence so that it has a similar meaning to the first sentence, using the word given. **Do not change the word given.** You must use between **three** and **six** words, including the word given. Here is an example **(0)**.

Example:

0 Fernanda refused to wear her sister's old dress.

NOT

Fernanda said that .... her sister's old dress.

The gap can be filled with the words 'she would not wear', so you write:

Example:	**0**	SHE WOULD NOT WEAR

Write the missing words **IN CAPITAL LETTERS on the separate answer sheet**.

---

43 Sally was all ready to leave the office when her boss asked her to type up a report.

POINT

Sally was .... the office when her boss asked her to type up a report.

44 Mark once worked for an international charity organisation on a voluntary basis.

AS

Mark used .... with an international charity organisation.

45 They plan to repair the bridge this weekend.

SCHEDULED

The repair of the bridge .... place this weekend.

46 If you change any of these arrangements, please be sure to let us know.

NOTIFY

Please ensure that .... change in these arrangements.

47 Most of the problems arose because there was no leadership on the committee.

CAUSED

It was the .... most of the problems on the committee.

48 I didn't realise that she had decided to come to the meeting.

DECISION

I was unaware .... attend the meeting.

49 I'm going to eat less chocolate this year.

DOWN

I'm going to .... of chocolate I eat this year.

50 We got started on the new project immediately.

TIME

We lost .... on the new project.

PAPER 4   LISTENING (approximately 40 minutes)

Part 1

You will hear three different extracts. For questions **1–6**, choose the answer (**A**, **B** or **C**) which fits best according to what you hear. There are two questions for each extract.

Extract One

You hear part of a radio discussion about a football team.

1   What impresses the man about the player called John Elliott?

    A   He is able to keep calm when he gets near the goal area.

    B   He is good at preventing the opponents from scoring.

    C   He can score many goals given the right conditions.

2   What do the two speakers disagree about?

    A   the inflated price paid for the new player

    B   the new player's long-term prospects in the team

    C   the manager's previous mistakes when purchasing players

Extract Two

You hear part of a radio interview with Deanna Carriconde, who has just won a prize for her environmental work in South America.

3   Deanna thinks the underlying cause of the ecosystem changes she mentions is

    A   overfishing by industrial fisheries.

    B   increased local sea temperatures.

    C   growth of predator populations in the area.

4   How do the local fishermen feel about Deanna's work now?

    A   unhappy about sharing their catch with marine creatures she protects

    B   pleased that she has prevented industrial exploitation of anchovies

    C   optimistic about the prospect of catching better quality fish

Extract Three

You hear part of a radio programme about books and reading.

5 Why did the woman read the book she describes?

    A It was an unexpected gift.

    B She came across it by chance.

    C It was recommended to her.

6 What did the book help her to understand?

    A how strange the world is

    B how enjoyable stories can be

    C how she could become a writer

Part 2

You will hear part of a radio programme about cherries, small fruit which grow on trees. For questions **7–14**, complete the sentences.

CHERRIES

The speaker gives the example of

| | 7 | as a crop being replaced by cherries.

To protect young trees from extremes of weather, a

| | 8 | may be used.

Cherries are prone to cracking because there is hardly any

| | 9 | on the skin of the fruit.

The speaker compares the cherry to a | | 10 | when explaining

the effect of rain on the fruit.

Shoppers are advised to purchase cherries which have a

| | 11 | stem and look fresh and tasty.

The traditional view was that cherries need up to

| | 12 | before they produce a useful crop.

The most popular new variety of cherry tree amongst farmers has the name

| | 13 |

While picking cherries, keep a

| | 14 | in your mouth to stop you eating too many.

Part 3

You will hear a radio interview in which an artist called Sophie Axel is talking about her life and career. For questions **15–20**, choose the answer (**A, B, C** or **D**) which fits best according to what you hear.

15 Sophie illustrates the importance of colour in her life by saying she

    A has coloured daydreams.
    B associates letters and colours.
    C paints people in particular colours.
    D links colours with days of the week.

16 Sophie's attitude to risk is that her children should be

    A left to cope with it.
    B warned about it.
    C taught how to deal with it.
    D protected from it.

17 Sophie's mother and aunt use their artistic gifts professionally in the

    A pictures they paint together.
    B plays they perform on stage.
    C objects they help to create.
    D clothes they design and make.

18 Sophie feels the puppet show she mentions is a good example of

    A the inspiration she gives to other people.
    B the admiration she now enjoys.
    C the expectations she has to live up to.
    D the assistance she gives the playgroup.

19 Sophie was a failure at art school because she

    A was not interested in design.
    B favoured introspective painting.
    C was very pessimistic.
    D had a different approach to art.

20 When Sophie had no money to repair her bike, she offered to

    A take a part-time job.
    B publicise a national charity.
    C produce an advertisement.
    D design posters on commission.

Part 4

You will hear five short extracts in which people are talking about tourism.

TASK ONE

For questions **21–25**, choose from the list **A–H** each speaker's occupation.

TASK TWO

For questions **26–30**, choose from the list **A–H** each speaker's aim for the future.

While you listen you must complete both tasks.

A travel broadcaster	**A** to increase the amount spent by clients
B hotel owner	**B** to improve our circulation
C guide book publisher	**C** to revive country skills
D tourist board representative	**D** to raise standards overall
E environmentalist	**E** to restore local transport networks
F railway executive	**F** to refurbish the rooms
G manager of a tourist attraction	**G** to attract a new type of client
H local government official	**H** to expand tourist accommodation

Speaker 1	21		Speaker 1	26
Speaker 2	22		Speaker 2	27
Speaker 3	23		Speaker 3	28
Speaker 4	24		Speaker 4	29
Speaker 5	25		Speaker 5	30

PAPER 5 SPEAKING (15 minutes)

There are two examiners. One (the interlocutor) conducts the test, providing you with the necessary materials and explaining what you have to do. The other examiner (the assessor) is introduced to you, but then takes no further part in the interaction.

Part 1 (3 minutes)

The interlocutor first asks you and your partner a few questions. The interlocutor asks candidates for some information about themselves, then widens the scope of the questions by asking about, e.g. candidates' leisure activities, studies, travel and daily life. Candidates are expected to respond to the interlocutor's questions, and listen to what their partner has to say.

Part 2 (a one-minute 'long turn' for each candidate, plus 30-second response from the second candidate)

You are each given the opportunity to talk for about a minute, and to comment briefly after your partner has spoken.

The interlocutor gives you a set of pictures and asks you to talk about them for about one minute. It is important to listen carefully to the interlocutor's instructions. The interlocutor then asks your partner a question about your pictures and your partner responds briefly.

You are then given another set of pictures to look at. Your partner talks about these pictures for about one minute. This time the interlocutor asks you a question about your partner's pictures and you respond briefly.

Part 3 (approximately 4 minutes)

In this part of the test you and your partner are asked to talk together. The interlocutor places a new set of pictures on the table between you. This stimulus provides the basis for a discussion.

The interlocutor explains what you have to do.

Part 4 (approximately 4 minutes)

The interlocutor asks some further questions, which leads to a more general discussion of what you have talked about in Part 3. You may comment on your partner's answers if you wish.

Paper 5 frames

Test 1

Note: In the examination, there will be both an assessor and an interlocutor in the room. The visual material for **Test 1** appears on pages C1 and C2 (Part 2), and C3 (Part 3).

Part 1   3 minutes (5 minutes for groups of three)

Interlocutor: Good morning/afternoon/evening. My name is .... and this is my colleague ....

And your names are?

Can I have your mark sheets, please?

Thank you.

First of all we'd like to know something about you.

Select one or two questions and ask candidates in turn, as appropriate.

- Where are you from?
- What do you do here/there?
- How long have you been studying English?
- What do you enjoy most about learning English?

Select one or more questions from any of the following categories, as appropriate.

Learning

- Do you prefer studying on your own or with other people? (Why?)
- How important have teachers been in your life so far?

Places

- What is the most memorable place you have ever visited?
- Which is the most important room in your house? (Why is that?)

Health and fitness

- What do you do to keep fit?
- If you had the opportunity to learn a new sport, what would it be? (Why?)

Part 2   4 minutes (6 minutes for groups of three)

Flags

Wheels

Interlocutor:	In this part of the test, I'm going to give each of you three pictures. I'd like you to talk about them on your own for about a minute, and also to answer a question briefly about your partner's pictures.
	(Candidate A), it's your turn first. Here are your pictures. They show different situations in which flags are used.
	Indicate the pictures on page C1 to the candidates.
	I'd like you to compare two of the pictures, and say why the flags are being used, and what effect they might have on people who see them.
	All right?
Candidate A:	[*1 minute*]
Interlocutor:	Thank you.
	(Candidate B), in which picture do you think the flags have the greatest significance?
Candidate B:	[*Approximately 30 seconds*]
Interlocutor:	Thank you.
	Now, *(Candidate B)*, here are your pictures. They show people and different kinds of wheels.
	Indicate the pictures on page C2 to the candidates.
	I'd like you to compare two of the pictures, and say what the wheels enable people to do, and how important they might be.
	All right?
Candidate B:	[*1 minute*]
Interlocutor:	Thank you.
	(Candidate A), which wheel do you think would be the most difficult to operate?
Candidate A:	[*Approximately 30 seconds*]
Interlocutor:	Thank you.

Parts 3 and 4   8 minutes (12 minutes for groups of three)

Better health care

Part 3

Interlocutor:	Now, I'd like you to talk about something together for about three minutes. *(5 minutes for groups of three)*
	Here are some suggestions for improving health care in your area.
	Indicate the pictures on page C3 to the candidates.
	First, talk to each other about how effective these suggestions might be in improving health care. Then decide which two suggestions would benefit the local community most.
	All right?
Candidates:	[*3 minutes (5 minutes for groups of three)*]
Interlocutor:	Thank you.

Part 4

Interlocutor:	*Select any of the following questions as appropriate:*

- Some people say we rely too much on medicines nowadays. What's your opinion?
- Should children's health education be the responsibility of parents or schools? (Why?)
- What can be done to make hospitals more friendly places for young children?
- What in your view are the qualities of a good doctor?
- Do you think our lifestyles will become more healthy or less healthy in the future? (Why?)

Thank you. That is the end of the test.

Select any of the following prompts as appropriate:

- What do you think?
- Do you agree?
- How about you?

Test 2

Note: In the examination, there will be both an assessor and an interlocutor in the room.
The visual material for **Test 2** appears on pages C4, C5 (Part 2), and C6 (Part 3).

Part 1 3 minutes (5 minutes for groups of three)

Interlocutor: Good morning/afternoon/evening. My name is .... and this is my colleague ....

And your names are?

Can I have your mark sheets, please?

Thank you.

First of all we'd like to know something about you.

Select one or two questions and ask candidates in turn, as appropriate.

- Where are you from?
- What do you do here/there?
- How long have you been studying English?
- What do you enjoy most about learning English?

Select one or more questions from any of the following categories, as appropriate.

Daily life

- How important is the computer in your daily life?
- Is it easy for you to find time to relax every day? (Why? / Why not?)

Friends

- Do you and your friends share the same interests? (Is this a good thing?)
- Do you think you will still have the same friends in ten years' time?

The future

- What do you think you will be doing in five years' time?
- Are you excited or worried about the future? (Why?)

Part 2   4 minutes (6 minutes for groups of three)

Learning through games

Expressing feelings

Interlocutor: In this part of the test, I'm going to give each of you three pictures. I'd like you to talk about them on your own for about a minute, and also to answer a question briefly about your partner's pictures.

(Candidate A), it's your turn first. Here are your pictures. They show children playing different games.

Indicate the pictures on page C4 to the candidates.

I'd like you to compare two of the pictures, and say why children enjoy games like these, and what children might learn from playing them.

All right?

Candidate A: [*1 minute*]

Interlocutor: Thank you.

(Candidate B), which game do you think the children seem to be enjoying most?

Candidate B: [*Approximately 30 seconds*]

Interlocutor: Thank you.

Now, *(Candidate B)*, here are your pictures. They show people expressing different feelings.

Indicate the pictures on page C5 to the candidates.

I'd like you to compare two of the pictures, and say what feelings are being expressed, and what might have made the people feel like this.

All right?

Candidate B: [*1 minute*]

Interlocutor: Thank you.

(Candidate A), which picture do you think shows the person's feelings most clearly?

Candidate A: [*Approximately 30 seconds*]

Interlocutor: Thank you.

Parts 3 and 4   8 minutes (12 minutes for groups of three)

Attracting passengers

Part 3

Interlocutor:	Now, I'd like you to talk about something together for about three minutes. *(5 minutes for groups of three)*
	Here are some ideas for improvements that an airline is considering as a way to attract more passengers.
	Indicate the pictures on page C6 to the candidates.
	First, talk to each other about how great the demand might be for these improvements. Then decide which would be the most, and which the least, effective in attracting more passengers.
	All right?
Candidates:	[*3 minutes (5 minutes for groups of three)*]
Interlocutor:	Thank you.

Part 4

Interlocutor:	*Select any of the following questions as appropriate:*

- Should people get to know their own countries before travelling abroad? (Why? / Why not?)
- What do you think is the best age for young people to start travelling abroad? (Why?)
- What problems do people have travelling around large cities?
- Which kinds of transport do you think might disappear in the future?
- Some people say there is nowhere left to explore on this planet. What's your opinion?

Thank you. That is the end of the test.

Select any of the following prompts as appropriate:

- What do you think?
- Do you agree?
- How about you?

Test 3

Note: In the examination, there will be both an assessor and an interlocutor in the room. The visual material for **Test 3** appears on pages C7 and C8 (Part 2), and C9 (Part 3).

Part 1   3 minutes (5 minutes for groups of three)

Interlocutor: Good morning/afternoon/evening. My name is .... and this is my colleague ....

And your names are?

Can I have your mark sheets, please?

Thank you.

First of all we'd like to know something about you.

Select one or two questions and ask candidates in turn, as appropriate.

- Where are you from?
- What do you do here/there?
- How long have you been studying English?
- What do you enjoy most about learning English?

Select one or more questions from any of the following categories, as appropriate.

Leisure

- What do you do to relax after a busy day?
- How important is music in your life?

Travel

- Where would you like to go for your next holiday? (Why?)
- What do you enjoy most about being on holiday?

People

- Who has had the greatest influence on your life so far?
- How easy is it for you to meet new people?

Part 2   4 minutes (6 minutes for groups of three)

Storing things

Retail outlets

Interlocutor:	In this part of the test, I'm going to give each of you three pictures. I'd like you to talk about them on your own for about a minute, and also to answer a question briefly about your partner's pictures.
	(Candidate A), it's your turn first. Here are your pictures. They show ways of storing things.
	Indicate the pictures on page C7 to the candidates.
	I'd like you to compare two of the pictures, and say how practical it is to store things in these ways, and how easy it might be for people to find what they are looking for.
	All right?
Candidate A:	[*1 minute*]
Interlocutor:	Thank you.
	(Candidate B), which way of storing things do you think is the most practical?
Candidate B:	[*Approximately 30 seconds*]
Interlocutor:	Thank you.
	Now, *(Candidate B)*, here are your pictures. They show different places to shop.
	Indicate the pictures on page C8 to the candidates.
	I'd like you to compare two of the pictures, and say what kind of customers they might attract, and what the advantages of shopping in these places might be.
	All right?
Candidate B:	[*1 minute*]
Interlocutor:	Thank you.
	(Candidate A), which of these places do you think offers the best value for money?
Candidate A:	[*Approximately 30 seconds*]
Interlocutor:	Thank you.

Parts 3 and 4   8 minutes (12 minutes for groups of three)

Weather conditions

Part 3

Interlocutor:	Now, I'd like you to talk about something together for about three minutes. *(5 minutes for groups of three)*
	Here are some pictures showing different kinds of weather conditions in the world.
	Indicate the pictures on page C9 to the candidates.
	First, talk to each other about how the weather conditions can affect people's lives. Then decide which two kinds of weather could have the most harmful effects.
	All right?
Candidates:	[*3 minutes (5 minutes for groups of three)*]
Interlocutor:	Thank you.

Part 4

Interlocutor: *Select any of the following questions as appropriate:*

- What effect does a country's climate have on the personality of the people living there?
- What advantages or disadvantages are there in living in a country which has seasons?
- Some people's idea of happiness is a lazy summer's day. Why do you think this is?
- Why do people spend time sunbathing when they are told it is so bad for their health?
- Some people say more should be done to prevent global warming. What's your opinion?

Thank you. That is the end of the test.

Select any of the following prompts as appropriate:

- What do you think?
- Do you agree?
- How about you?

Test 4

Note: In the examination, there will be both an assessor and an interlocutor in the room.
The visual material for **Test 4** appears on pages C10 and C11 (Part 2), and C12 (Part 3).

Part 1   3 minutes (5 minutes for groups of three)

Interlocutor: Good morning/afternoon/evening. My name is .... and this is my
colleague ....

And your names are?

Can I have your mark sheets, please?

Thank you.

First of all we'd like to know something about you.

*Select one or two questions and ask candidates in turn, as
appropriate.*

- Where are you from?
- What do you do here/there?
- How long have you been studying English?
- What do you enjoy most about learning English?

*Select one or more questions from any of the following categories,
as appropriate.*

Personal experience

- In what ways do you hope to use your English in the future?
- Looking back on your life, what has been a memorable event for
  you?

The media

- Do you prefer watching films at home or in the cinema? (Why?)
- How important are newspapers for you? (Why do you say that?)

Travel

- What advice would you give to someone coming to visit your
  country?
- Would you consider going on holiday on your own? (Why? /
  Why not?)

Part 2   4 minutes (6 minutes for groups of three)

Bygone days

Unexpected events

Interlocutor: In this part of the test, I'm going to give each of you three pictures. I'd like you to talk about them on your own for about a minute, and also to answer a question briefly about your partner's pictures.

(*Candidate A*), it's your turn first. Here are your pictures. They show people with photographs of the past.

Indicate the pictures on page C10 to the candidates.

I'd like you to compare two of the pictures, and say what aspects of the past the photographs show, and how the people might be feeling as they look back on the past.

All right?

Candidate A: [*1 minute*]

Interlocutor: Thank you.

(*Candidate B*) which of these people do you think might regret the passing of time the most?

Candidate B: [*Approximately 30 seconds*]

Interlocutor: Thank you.

Now, (*Candidate B*), here are your pictures. They show unexpected events.

Indicate the pictures on a page C11 to the candidates.

I'd like you to compare two of the pictures, and say what might have caused these events, and how they could have been prevented.

All right?

Candidate B: [*1 minute*]

Interlocutor: Thank you.

(*Candidate A*), which of these pictures do you think might appear in a national newspaper?

Candidate A: [*Approximately 30 seconds*]

Interlocutor: Thank you.

Parts 3 and 4   8 minutes (12 minutes for groups of three)

Relieving the pressure

Part 3

Interlocutor:	Now, I'd like you to talk about something together for about three minutes. (*5 minutes for groups of three*)
	Here are some pictures showing ways in which people can escape from the pressures of everyday life.
	Indicate the pictures on page C12 to the candidates.
	First, talk to each other about how these activities might help people escape from the pressures of everyday life. Then decide which two might have the most lasting benefit.
	All right?
Candidates:	[*3 minutes (5 minutes for groups of three)*]
Interlocutor:	Thank you.

Part 4

Interlocutor:	*Select any of the following questions as appropriate:*

- What other things help people to relax after a busy day?
- Do you think some people work better under pressure? (Why? / Why not?)
- Nowadays, many people work from home. Do you think this is a good or a bad thing? (Why?)
- Some people believe that any activity we do becomes boring after a while. What's your opinion?
- Is it possible to be totally happy in life? (Why? / Why not?)

Thank you. That is the end of the test.

Select any of the following prompts as appropriate:

- What do you think?
- Do you agree?
- How about you?

Marks and results

Paper 1 Reading

Candidates record their answers in pencil on a separate answer sheet. Two marks are given for each correct answer in **Parts 1, 2** and **3** and one mark is given for each correct answer in **Part 4**. The total score is then weighted to 40 marks for the whole Reading paper.

Paper 2 Writing

General impression mark scheme

A General Impression Mark Scheme is used in conjunction with a Task-specific Mark Scheme, which focuses on criteria specific to each particular task. The General Impression Mark Scheme summarises the content, organisation and cohesion, range of structures and vocabulary, register and format, and target reader indicated in each task.

A summary of the General Impression Mark Scheme is given below. Trained examiners, who are co-ordinated prior to each examination session, work with a more detailed version, which is subject to updating. The CAE General Impression Mark Scheme is interpreted at Council of Europe, Common European Framework Level C1.

* Candidates who do not address all the content points will be penalised for dealing inadequately with the requirements of the task. Candidates who fully satisfy the **Band 3** descriptor are likely to demonstrate an adequate performance at CAE level.

Band 5	For a **Band 5** to be awarded, the candidate's writing has a very positive effect on the target reader. The content is relevant* and the topic is fully developed. Information and ideas are skilfully organised through a range of cohesive devices, which are used to good effect. A wide range of complex structures and vocabulary is used effectively. Errors are minimal, and inaccuracies which do occur have no impact on communication. Register and format are consistently appropriate to the purpose of the task and the audience.
Band 4	For a **Band 4** to be awarded, the candidate's writing has a positive effect on the target reader. The content is relevant* and the topic is developed. Information and ideas are clearly organised through the use of a variety of cohesive devices. A good range of complex structures and vocabulary is used. Some errors may occur with vocabulary and when complex language is attempted, but these do not cause difficulty for the reader. Register and format are usually appropriate to the purpose of the task and the audience.
Band 3	For a **Band 3** to be awarded, the candidate's writing has a satisfactory effect on the target reader. The content is relevant* with some development of the topic. Information and ideas are generally organised logically, though cohesive devices may not always be used appropriately. A satisfactory range of structures and vocabulary is used, though word choice may lack precision. Errors which do occur do not cause difficulty for the reader. Register and format are reasonably appropriate to the purpose of the task and the audience.
Band 2	For a **Band 2** to be awarded, the candidate's writing has a negative effect on the target reader. The content is not always relevant. Information and ideas are inadequately organised and sometimes incoherent, with inaccurate use of cohesive devices. The range of structures and vocabulary is limited and/or repetitive, and errors may be basic or cause difficulty for the reader. Register and format are sometimes inappropriate to the purpose of the task and the audience.
Band 1	For a **Band 1** to be awarded, the candidate's writing has a very negative effect on the target reader. The content is often irrelevant. Information and ideas are poorly organised and often incoherent and there is minimal use of cohesive devices. The range of structures and vocabulary is severely limited, and errors frequently cause considerable difficulty for the reader. Register and format are often inappropriate to the purpose of the task and the audience.
Band 0	For a **Band zero** to be awarded, there is either too little language for assessment or the candidate's writing is totally irrelevant or illegible.

Paper 2 sample answers and examiner's comments

Sample A (Test 1, Question 1 – Report)

> To: College Principal
>
> From: Student Annette Fournier
>
> Topic: Career Conference Attended
>
> As requested, I am submitting a report about this conference we attended last weekend at Vancouver Hall expressing our points of views about this event.
>
> The conference was opened on Friday at 9.00 a.m. and the opening ceremony was crowded with professors and students from different colleges from all over Canada. The following days we attended the exhibitions exposed, even though there were talks on wide range of careers, it was very difficult to find experts available to give advice about specific jobs. There were over 100 different jobs, however, for us it was impossible to change ideas with a specialized person in languages.
>
> Despite this fact, the exhibition was great, some of the talks were amazingly good especially the ones about science, we learnt a lot about this field.
>
> A good idea would be that for the forthcoming exhibitions more humanities experts would attend the conference and also organizers should try to get enough people to answer questions.
>
> In summary we could say it was an excellent opportunity for us to share with several kind of students and an extraordinary way to get knowledge about so many careers that will enhance our future studies.

Comments

Content (points covered)
The task has been completed and all the necessary points are covered with some expansion.

Organisation and cohesion
Some attempt has been made to use an appropriate format.

Range
The range of language is satisfactory with a good range of vocabulary.

Accuracy
The writing is generally accurate although occasionally the wrong word was chosen (e.g. you exchange ideas . . . (not *change* ideas), and the word *exposed* is used inappropriately). The candidate needs to pay some attention to punctuation, particularly to the use of the comma, as inappropriate use of punctuation occasionally makes it hard to follow the writing.

Appropriacy of register and format
The register used is generally appropriate although it would be better to put relatively informal comments like 'the exhibition was great' into less colloquial language for a report to the college principal.

Target reader
The target reader would be informed as to how the writer felt about the conference. However, occasional comments are made about how to improve the conference that would be more relevant for the conference organisers than the writer's own college principal.

Band 4

Sample B (Test 1, Question 2 – Article)

Is there a deeper meaning behind fashion?

Nowadays, a lot of people think talking about clothes and fashion is superficial because it's only about looks and not about someone's character or personality. But it's not!

Fashion isn't only about looking as good as a supermodel. It's much more than that because the clothes people wear can tell you something about their character or the society or culture they come from. Let me give you an example. In the Golden Twenties women in Germany became more independent and decided to enjoy life more for example by going to cafes and bars. And what did they do? They cut their hair and wore extravagant dresses to express their new attitudes to life.

Another example is the 21st century woman who tends to wear trousers rather than skirts or dresses as her grandmother used to do. Why? The reason is, that she wants to express her independence as a working woman who needs to wear comfortable and practical clothes and she also wants to be treated equally as men.

It is important to know that people's clothes indicate the culture or society they come from. What's more, clothes can also tell you interesting things about people's lifestyles for example in which business they work or if they are environmentalist. The colour of the clothes someone is wearing might reflect his/her mood.

So the next time you walk down a road keep your eyes open and you'll be surprised how much you can learn about people's identities. Just like in the saying 'you are what you wear.'

Comments

Content (points covered)
Task fully completed, with appropriate expansion.

Organisation and cohesion
Clearly organised with good use of cohesive devices.

Range
Wide range of vocabulary and structure.

Accuracy
Controlled and natural use of language with minimal errors.

Appropriacy of register and format
Consistently appropriate throughout.

Target reader
Very positive effect on target reader, who would consider publishing the article.

Band 5

Sample C (Test 1, Question 3 – Contribution)

One of the most popular TV programmes in my country is 'electing' Miss Lebanon. Three years ago, it shared its popularity with other game programmes, but now, thanks to a new version presented in the programme, other programmes seem uncomparable to Miss Lebanon.

The lucky girl to win is not elected by any referees. In fact, people vote for their girl. Just like many others programmes that used this method, the candidates are take to a house, where they are completely isolated and banned from going out. The only connection between the girls and the 'external world' is the telephone. The house, with all its rooms and facilities, is equiped with cameras that films all their actions and records what they say. The film is then broadcasted on TV and the audience are given one hour to vote for their candidate via telephones, text messaging, or the internet. Each week the girl with less votes leaves and after several weeks, we have a miss Lebanon.

The programme gained its popularity not only because of its virtuality, but because it motivates people's curiousity to look through to other people's lives and personal affairs. So, what about those people being observed all the time? More interesting, they are beautiful girls who are seen daily 'naturaly' because they can't control their every action or word. Each of us wonders if everybody lives the same life as; same problems, interests, or any other concept of living and treating others.

I personaly don't think that this programme deserves its popularity because it intrudes people's lives (though they permit that) and from my perspective it's a waste of time, and it seems to me a boring programme to watch. I hate being watched or following rules and besides, who is so interested in watching my life?! Even their lives is not worth watching because all they do is wondering the house talking, eating, sleeping, and finally, one of them gets the crown. Nothing really interesting.

Comments

Content (points covered)
All points covered. Ambitious attempt at task.

Organisation and cohesion
Clearly organised into paragraphs. Good internal cohesion.

Range
Good range of vocabulary and structure.

Accuracy
A number of non-impeding errors (e.g. 'equiped with cameras that films', 'the candidates are take').

Appropriacy of register and format
Consistently appropriate.

Target reader
Would be informed and interested.

Band 3

Sample D (Test 2, Question 5a – Review)

> I highly recommend you to read Lucky Jim. It is a very funny story. Lucky Jim teaches history at university. He is afraid to loose his work and so he try very hard to be nice to his boss. He doesn't like this man or his son, Bertrand and he doesn't like the other professors too, also his girlfriend who teaches at same university. He has another relation with Christine who is really the girlfriend of Bertrand. A very funny part of the story is when Lucky Jim must make an important lecture. He feels very worried about make this lecture and drinks too much alcool. Then in his lecture he tells what he really thinks of his boss and the other professors. Of course, he then looses his job. But he gets a lot better job in London with more money. Christine leaves Bertrand for him and one day they meet his former boss on the street and they just laugh at him. Lucky Jim is not a very likable person. He is not honest man and he is not kind person. But he is certainly lucky man and his story is very funny and very well written. To sum up, I enjoyed reading the book and I even laughed aloud when I was reading.

Comments

Content (points covered)
The candidate does not deal with one of the main points of the task in that it does not describe a likeable character in the story. As a result, it is not possible for this answer to get a higher mark than 2.

Organisation and cohesion
The candidate has only written one paragraph – although it is certainly a clearly constructed paragraph, making some use of appropriate connecting devices.

Range
A satisfactory range of vocabulary is used.

Accuracy
The candidate writes reasonably accurately although the words *lose*, *alcohol*, *likeable* and *written* are not spelt correctly.

Appropriacy of register and format
Register and format are appropriate.

Target reader
Would be informed about the plot of the story and about the candidate's opinion of it but would not know which character the candidate found likeable and why.

Band 2

Sample E (Test 2, Question 5b – Essay)

> *The Pelican Brief is very good book of John Grisham. It is also a very great film with Julia Roberts and Denzel Washington. Julia Roberts is one of my favourite actor and she play very well part of heroine, who is law student. In the story this heroine lawer tries to discover why two judges murdered. She soon understands that politics, including President of USA, and big business are involved for the crime and she is also almost murdered several times. In the end a journalist helps her to find the truth.*
>
> *The story is called The Pelican Brief because at the centre of the story is some land where pelicans live. Big business want to destroy this land. A brief are instructions for a job for a lawer or some other person. So the heroine's brief is that she should find out the reason of the murder of the judges. And that reason is the pelicans' land which both judges wanted to keep for the pelicans. Business wanted to develop the land. So the judges were killed.*
>
> *In conclusion, The Pelican Brief is a very exciting story and I enjoied read it very much. I absolutely recommend that people should read it even they already have seen the film. When I read it, I didn't want to stop to read it and I couldn't put it down untill I finished it.*

Comments

Content (points covered)
The content is relevant and all the aspects of the task are addressed.

Organisation and cohesion
The writing is organised in clear paragraphs and there is some attempt at using cohesive devices.

Range
A satisfactory range of vocabulary is used although there is a certain lack of precision with the use of such words as *good*, *great* and *well*. It would be better to avoid the repetition of *read* in the last paragraph if at all possible.

Accuracy
The candidate makes some errors – *lawyer*, *enjoyed* and *until* are all spelt wrongly, for example. Also there are a couple of examples of the verb not agreeing with its subject and of the wrong choice of preposition. These and other errors do not interfere with communication.

Appropriacy of register and format
Register and format are generally appropriate although occasionally the writing feels a little informal for an essay.

Target reader
Would be informed about the reason for the title of *The Pelican Brief* and about the candidate's opinion of the story.

Band 3

Sample F (Test 3, Question 3 – Competition entry)

The Best Teacher

What do a teacher need to be the best?
Well first of all he does not only have to know about the subject he is teaching but to know a little bit of every subject General Culture.

He also has to be patient, polite but at the same time strict when it comes to do the student not only memorize but learn.

The wisdom the best teacher needs has to be of great value because he is in charge of a great assignment to lead young people into the right way, fill with knowledge those minds that are starting to learn and to wake up to the world.

He needs to teach as well as chemistry, science, arts, literature, etc, he has to teach them moral but more important to be human.

That's a good teacher and that is the kind of teacher I have, his name is xxxxxx and he is my current philosophy teacher. He is a realistic day dreamer who is always looking for the truth and good values in the world. He is not only a philosopher teacher, he have a degree in Physics. You can talk with him for hours about pretty much any subject, he can become your best friend but he is your critic as well. With the phrase 'Not because I am your friend I am going to lie you' he can help understand your mistakes and grow.

He has taught me the importance of life, the importance of wanted to be curious all the time, to look for answers no matter how silly my question is, to see everything with an object point of view but also to be a dreamer as him, to be imaginative and creative.

The influence he has on me is of huge importance, he is the reason I want to do a Master on Philosophy. He is for me and for all the people he had taught the best teacher ever, so vote for him because he deserves it.

Comments

Content (points covered)
All points addressed but not developed. Some generalisation at the beginning, but linked to task.

Organisation and cohesion
Some good attempts at organisation but over-paragraphed. Little evidence of internal cohesion.

Range
Attempt at range marred by errors.

Accuracy
Some impeding errors (e.g. *He needs to teach as well as chemistry*).

Appropriacy of register and format
Consistent and appropriate.

Target reader
Would have a negative effect on target reader.

Band 2

Sample G (Test 4, Question 1 – Proposal)

From: Peter Keller
To: Ms D. Jackson
Subject: Proposal on library facilities

The aim of this report is to present according to the actual library condition some suggestions to improve and make an advice on which are the important and necessary needs.

Time and Space
First of all, the library's schedule means a great disadvantage to the students. As the length of time it is open is not enough and so many students do not finish their asigments.

    Then, although the work space is confortable, certainly it is not plenty of space so it gets crowded easily.

Reading and Watching
The library has a wide variety of books in all themes and subjects. However, the videos, that are some documentaries about history and science, are not really useful. They are old and non-up-dated, causing annoying reactions to that. A requested reading object are English magazines that are compulsory to certain projects.

Conclusion
The most important things to improve are the workplace, we feel that when you have to deal with studies, asigments, projects, the place where you do it should be agreeable, quiet that helps you to concentrated and focused yourself. To sum up, the library should have a workplace, a bit bigger and quiet.

Comments

Content (points covered)
A reasonable attempt at the task. All the points are addressed.

Organisation and cohesion
Clearly organised with useful headings.

Range
The range is satisfactory.

Accuracy
Fairly accurate but errors are made when longer, more complex sentences are attempted. Some spelling errors e.g. *it should be comfortable* (not *confortable*) and *assignment* (not *asigment*). Also occasionally the wrong word is chosen; for example, it should be *current* (not *actual*) *condition* and *give some advice* (not *make an advice*). Although occasionally the writer does not choose the most natural word, his meaning is always clear.

Appropriacy of register and format
The register used is appropriately and consistently neutral.

Target reader
The target reader would be informed as to what the writer feels is the most important way in which facilities could be improved.

Band 3

Sample H (Test 4, Question 4 – Letter of application)

> Dear Sir/Madam
>
> I am writing in response to your announcement, recently published in an issue of the "Daily Planet". I am really interested in participating in your new television programme.
>
> To begin with, I would like to put forward some information about myself. I am 20 years old and I am currently studying the Law in the university of Athens. I have been studying both English and French since I was 12. Consequently it would be easy for me to communicate with the rest of the group.
>
> Furthermore, I have joined a climbing team since 1998 and I have taken part in many activities such as climbing up mountain Olympus twice or climbing up mountain Rodopi. Moreover, I have been in the basket-ball team of my high-school for three years where we were champions for three times in the local championships. It is obvious that my physical skills and my body strength are bound to help me to survive under difficult circumstances during my stay on a remoted island.
>
> As far as my personality is concerned, I do believe that I am very polite and honest with people. I have great communicational skills and this derives from the fact that I am used to be a member of different sports groups. My experience in climbing mountain Olympus, has supplied me with a great ammount of patience. I am always willing to offer my help and experience to less-experienced team-mates and to give any piece of advice. Should be important.
>
> I strongly believe that I am the perfect candidate for this enthralling television programme. I really indulge myself in being under difficult conditions, supplied only with the basic objects. It seems to me that it is an outlet for my energy.
>
> I enclose my curriculum vitae and a photographs. I would like to thank you in advance for considering my application. It would be a great pleasure for me to attend an interview and to supply you with further information, if required. I am looking forward to your prompt reply.

Comments

Content (points covered)
All points covered and developed.

Organisation and cohesion
Clearly organised into paragraphs with very good linking.

Range
Evidence of range of vocabulary and structure.

Accuracy
Some errors, mostly when complex language is attempted (*I am used to be a member* . . .).

Appropriacy of register and format
Consistent.

Target reader
Positive effect on target reader.

Band 4

Paper 3   Use of English

One mark is given for each correct answer in **Parts 1, 2** and **3**. Two marks are given for each correct answer in **Part 4**. For **Part 5**, candidates are awarded a mark of 2, 1 or 0 for each question according to the accuracy of their response. Correct spelling is required in **Parts 2, 3, 4** and **5**. The total mark is subsequently weighted to 40.

Paper 4   Listening

One mark is given for each correct answer. The total is weighted to give a mark out of 40 for the paper.

For security reasons, several versions of the Listening paper are used at each administration of the examination. Before grading, the performance of the candidates in each of the versions is compared and marks adjusted to compensate for any imbalance in levels of difficulty.

Paper 5   Speaking

Candidates are assessed on their own individual performance and not in relation to each other, according to the following five analytical criteria: grammatical resource, vocabulary resource, discourse management, pronunciation and interactive communication. Assessment is based on performance in the whole test and not in particular parts of the test.

Both examiners assess the candidates. The assessor applies detailed analytical scales, and the interlocutor applies a global achievement scale, which is based on the analytical scales.

Analytical scales

Grammatical resource

This refers to the accurate and appropriate use of a range of both simple and complex forms. Performance is viewed in terms of the overall effectiveness of the language used in spoken interaction.

Vocabulary resource

This refers to the candidate's ability to use a wide range of vocabulary to meet task requirements. At CAE level, the tasks require candidates to speculate and exchange views on unfamiliar topics. Performance is viewed in terms of the overall effectiveness of the language used in spoken interaction.

Discourse management

This refers to the candidate's ability to link utterances together to form coherent speech, without undue hesitation. The utterances should be relevant to the tasks and should be arranged logically to develop the themes or arguments required by the tasks.

Pronunciation

This refers to the candidate's ability to produce intelligible utterances to fulfil the task requirements. This includes stress and intonation as well as individual sounds. Examiners put themselves in the position of the non-ESOL specialist and assess the overall impact of the pronunciation and the degree of effort required to understand the candidate.

Interactive communication

This refers to the candidate's ability to take an active part in the development of the discourse. This requires the ability to participate in the range of interactive situations in the test and to develop discussions on a range of topics by initiating and responding appropriately. This also refers to the deployment of strategies to maintain interaction at an appropriate level throughout the test so that the tasks can be fulfilled.

Global achievement

This refers to the candidate's overall effectiveness in dealing with the tasks in the four separate parts of the CAE Speaking test. The global mark is an independent, impression mark which reflects the assessment of the candidate's performance from the interlocutor's perspective.

Marks

Marks for each of the criteria are awarded out of a nine-point scale. Marks for the Speaking test are subsequently weighted to produce a final mark out of 40.

CAE typical minimum adequate performance

The candidate develops the interaction with contributions which are mostly coherent and extended when dealing with the CAE level tasks. Grammar is mostly accurate and vocabulary appropriate. Utterances are understood with very little strain on the listener.

Test 1 Key

Paper 1   Reading (1 hour 15 minutes)

Part 1

1 A   2 C   3 D   4 A   5 D   6 A

Part 2

7 D   8 F   9 A   10 G   11 E   12 B

Part 3

13 B   14 C   15 B   16 B   17 D   18 A   19 A

Part 4

20 D   21 B   22 E   23 A   24 A   25 D   26 E   27 B   28 C   29 E
30 B   31 C   32 E   33 D   34 A

Paper 2   Writing (1 hour 30 minutes)

Task-specific Mark Schemes

Part 1

Question 1

Content (points covered)
For Band 3 or above, the candidate's **report** must:
• say how useful the careers conference was
• make recommendations about next year.

Organisation and cohesion
Clearly organised in paragraphs.
Report format.

Range
Language of description and recommendation.
Vocabulary related to careers.

Appropriacy of register and format
Unmarked or formal.

Target reader
Would be informed.

Part 2

Question 2

Content (points covered)
For Band 3 or above, the candidate's **article** must:
• agree or disagree that fashion reflects changes in society

- describe how fashion has changed since a time in the past
- describe any social changes this reveals.

Organisation and cohesion
Clearly organised in paragraphs with appropriate linking.

Range
Fashion-related vocabulary.
Language of description and opinion.

Appropriacy of register and format
May mix register if appropriate to approach taken by candidate.

Target reader
Would be informed and consider publishing the article.

Question 3

Content (points covered)
For Band 3 or above, the candidate's **contribution** must:
- identify and describe the most popular TV programme
- explain why the programme is so popular
- say whether the programme deserves popularity.
NB country need not be named.

Organisation and cohesion
Clear paragraphing.
Appropriate use of linking.

Range
Vocabulary of TV and entertainment.
Language of description, evaluation and opinion.

Appropriacy of register and format
Any, as long as consistent.

Target reader
Would be informed.

Question 4

Content (points covered)
For Band 3 or above, the candidate's **proposal** must:
- outline existing facilities
- explain how they could be improved.
NB candidates must make reference to both transport and housing.

Organisation and cohesion
Clear organisation of main parts.
Headings an advantage.
Letter, report or memo format acceptable.

Range
Language of description, explanation and evaluation.

Appropriacy of register and format
Formal or unmarked.

Target reader
Would be informed and consider the proposal.

Question 5 (a)

Content (points covered)
For Band 3 or above, the candidate's **report** must:
• outline the plot of *Lucky Jim*
• explain why it would be a good story to study in class.

Organisation and cohesion
Clearly organised into paragraphs with appropriate linking devices.
Headings may be an advantage.

Range
Language of narration, recommendation and opinion.
Vocabulary related to the plot of *Lucky Jim*.

Appropriacy of register and format
Any, as long as consistent.

Target reader
Would be informed and would be persuaded that *Lucky Jim* would be an appropriate choice for a text to study in class.

Question 5 (b)

Content (points covered)
For Band 3 or above, the candidate's **essay** must:
• name the person whom the candidate considers the most corrupt character in *The Pelican Brief*
• explain why the candidate holds this opinion.

Organisation and cohesion
Clearly organised into paragraphs with appropriate linking devices.

Range
Language of description, evaluation and opinion.
Vocabulary related to character description.

Appropriacy of register and format
Formal to unmarked.
Must be consistent.

Target reader
Would be informed both about the character chosen and the candidate's opinion of him or her.

Paper 3   Use of English (1 hour)

Part 1

1 A   2 B   3 D   4 B   5 A   6 C   7 A   8 B   9 D   10 A   11 D   12 A

Part 2

13 or / and   14 a   15 for   16 so / less / two   17 are   18 as   19 during / in /
throughout   20 There   21 on   22 much   23 What   24 such   25 down
26 which   27 of

Part 3

28 influential   29 attention   30 essentially   31 significance   32 awareness
33 knowledge   34 involvement   35 mysterious   36 evidence   37 undoubtedly / doubtless

Part 4

38 loose   39 slipped   40 head   41 ran   42 spot

Part 5

43 he'd / he would I rather not   44 denied I having seen   45 spent five minutes I looking / searching   46 will be I followed by   47 pleasure I to take you on / for a   48 in spite of I never having / having never   49 to be unable I to keep   50 to get my passport I renewed

Paper 4 Listening (approximately 40 minutes)

Part 1

1 B   2 A   3 C   4 C   5 C   6 B

Part 2

7 waterfall   8 road   9 hot, wet (in either order)   10 path   11 meat, vegetables (in either order)   12 energy   13 worried   14 $30 / 30 dollars / thirty dollars

Part 3

15 D   16 B   17 A   18 B   19 C   20 D

Part 4

21 B   22 E   23 C   24 G   25 F   26 G   27 A   28 H   29 D   30 C

Transcript	*This is the Cambridge Certificate in Advanced English Listening Test. Test One.*
	I'm going to give you the instructions for this test. I'll introduce each part of the test and give you time to look at the questions.
	At the start of each piece you'll hear this sound:
	tone
	You'll hear each piece twice.
	Remember, while you're listening, write your answers on the **question paper.** *You'll have* **five minutes** *at the end of the test to* **copy your answers onto the separate answer sheet.**
	There'll now be a pause. Please ask any questions now, because you must not speak during the test.
	[pause]
PART 1	*Now open your question paper and look at Part One.*
	[pause]
	You'll hear three different extracts. For questions one to six, choose the answer (A, B or C) which fits best according to what you hear. There are two questions for each extract.

Extract 1

You hear part of an interview with a woman who works in retail management. Now look at questions one and two.

[pause]

tone

Interviewer: So, Fiona, can you tell me about how you started in fashion retailing?
Fiona: Yes, of course. After I finished university, I took a job with a big high street chain – I was an assistant manager. Every week you would see the sales figures for your product and then act on that by placing repeat orders or putting a new style in. It was a good grounding. However, most of the staff had been there years and I think I did make mistakes in my dealings with them – I blush now to think of my time there. I then moved on, after five years, to my present job.
Interviewer: And now you're thinking of moving up the ladder. How do you see yourself in ten years' time?
Fiona: I would eventually like to be in senior management.
Interviewer: Well, before you rush off to see your line manager, I think you need to work out skills you can offer emphasising your selling points, showing them what you can do. Also have you been going the extra mile to get things done or doing more than what is asked of you, recently?

[pause]

tone

Now you'll hear the recording again.

[The recording is repeated.]

[pause]

Extract 2

You overhear a woman telling a friend a story about a swan. Now look at questions three and four.

[pause]

tone

Friend: So, what happened last weekend?
Woman: Well, we were taking our boat along the river, when we passed a pair of swans, with a nest nearby. One swan just carried on feeding, but the other one – the male I think – decided to come and investigate.
Friend: Oh, fantastic. I've never seen a swan's nest close up. I expect he was hungry.
Woman: Well, actually it was immediately obvious from his body language that he had other things on his mind. He was flapping his wings really hard, and approaching at incredible speed. And I guess we'd gone too close to the nest. I'd never have done that if I'd known what would happen.
Friend: Gosh, amazing. I've never heard of swans behaving like that before. So what did you do? Row like mad?
Woman: Well, we got out onto the bank, but he followed us up, and then stood between us and the boat for about an hour! We just couldn't frighten him away.
Friend: No, I suppose not. Still, I'm sure he wouldn't have hurt you.
Woman: Are you kidding? You should have seen the way he moved – swans can be really aggressive at nesting times.
Friend: Hmmm.

[pause]

tone

Now you'll hear the recording again.

[The recording is repeated.]

[pause]

<table>
<tr><td>*Extract 3*</td><td>*You hear part of an interview with Bruce Loader, a successful businessman who is talking about his early life. Now look at questions five and six.*</td></tr>
</table>

Extract 3   *You hear part of an interview with Bruce Loader, a successful businessman who is talking about his early life. Now look at questions five and six.*

[pause]

tone

Interviewer:	Bruce, at school, you discovered you had a natural talent for art.
Bruce:	Yes, I inherited my dad's gift for drawing. I wanted to do representational art; paint portraits. But every college I went to – and there were three who accepted me – all the college tutors said, 'Forget representational art, get a single lens reflex 33-millimetre camera, hit the shutter, crash, there's your picture. Not even Rembrandt could get that accuracy, so it's not worth it.'
Interviewer:	And you believed them?
Bruce:	I did. That was my biggest mistake. I haven't picked up a paintbrush since.
Interviewer:	How did your father react, when you told him you weren't going to art college?
Bruce:	His face was white with rage. He said, 'Right, that's it. You could have made something of going to college. You won't get another chance. Now I've got a perfectly good job for you on the factory floor. You start this week – take it or leave it.' I said, 'No, I'm going to start a business next.' He said, 'Well, at your own expense, then.'
Interviewer:	He refused to support you any more?
Bruce:	That's it, and so . . .

[pause]

tone

Now you'll hear the recording again.

[The recording is repeated.]

[pause]

That's the end of Part One.
Now turn to Part Two.

[pause]

PART 2   *Part Two*

You'll hear an explorer called Richard Livingstone talking about a trip he made in the rainforest of South America. For questions 7 to 14, complete the sentences. You now have 45 seconds to look at Part Two.

[pause]

tone

I'd set off, with my friend Matthew Price, to sail down a little-known river in the rainforest, in a homemade boat. Our original idea was to go all the way by boat, carrying it past any rough bits, but the river was much rockier and faster-flowing than we'd thought, which meant we were only covering a few kilometres each day. Then, suddenly, we realised that, as the river was about to go over a waterfall, we could go no further by boat.

As it was only a homemade thing, we decided to abandon it, and walk to the nearest road. As far as we knew, there were no villages or trading posts along the way and, on our map, it looked like a 100-kilometre walk.

And that walk, through thick rainforest with 25 kilos on our backs, was difficult. We walked for six days, it was hot and we were permanently wet through, before we came to any sign of civilisation. There were times when we really wondered if we'd ever get out of that jungle alive.

Then, on the seventh day, we suddenly came across a path – not an animal trail, but a man-made one, so we knew there must be people living there. It was going roughly in the right direction, so we followed it and, at dusk, we came to a deserted camp in a hollow. Deserted, but not uninhabited. There was digging equipment wrapped in plastic, alongside two water-filled holes. Obviously someone had been digging in search of gold at some time or another.

Nearby, on a rough wooden table, were some cooking utensils and a few other supplies, and whoever was camping there must've been intending to return soon because there was a large pot full of thick soup. We couldn't identify either the strange-looking pieces of meat or the unfamiliar vegetables it seemed to be made from, but we were in a desperate state. Over the previous seven days, we'd only had flour and rice to eat and, although we had plenty left, we were low on energy. This was our greatest problem.

So, we cooked up some of our rice and decided to have two spoonfuls from the pot with it. It was good, so we had another spoonful. And then another. Soon, nothing was left of our host's meal. Afterwards, we began to get worried. People living this sort of life could be very tough, and this one could return any minute. We decided to make an early start.

To show we were grateful, we placed 30 dollars in the cleaned-out cooking pot. It was quite a lot for the quantity of food – it was probably only worth 10 dollars or so – but that wasn't the point. This man wouldn't be able to pop to the supermarket to replace the food we'd eaten. But I have no regrets because that dinner gave us the strength to make it the rest of the way through the jungle safely.

[pause]

tone

Now you'll hear the recording again.

[The recording is repeated.]

[pause]

That's the end of Part Two.
Now turn to Part Three.

[pause]

PART 3   *Part Three*

You'll hear part of an interview with the astronaut Charles Duke, who is talking about his trip to the moon. For questions 15 to 20, choose the answer (A, B, C or D) which fits best according to what you hear. You now have one minute to look at Part Three.

[pause]

tone

Interviewer:	My guest today is Charles Duke, one of the few people to have walked on the moon as part of an Apollo mission. Charles, welcome to the studio. Have you always been hooked on space travel?
Charles:	Quite frankly, as a kid, it'd never entered my head. There wasn't even a space programme when I was young . . . so there weren't any astronauts.
Interviewer:	What about science fiction films at the cinema?
Charles:	I'd seen them, of course I used to wonder what space travel might be like – but it was never what you might describe as a fascination – if you follow me.
Interviewer:	So, how did it all come about?
Charles:	It was at the Naval Academy . . .
Interviewer:	Not in the Air Force?
Charles:	No, but I was a navy pilot. I had fallen in love with planes and nothing else would do. And that gave me the opportunity to start – to get selected for the astronaut programme.
Interviewer:	Presumably by then they were talking about putting rockets into space?
Charles:	Absolutely.
Interviewer:	And how did you find the training?
Charles:	I suppose the lunar surface training in the spacesuit was physically demanding in a way.
Interviewer:	Quite uncomfortable, I imagine.
Charles:	It's not what you might expect. Once the spacesuits get inflated, it gets very rigid. You had to fight to bend your arms and move your fingers inside the gloves.
Interviewer:	And how long did you spend inside it?
Charles:	Around four to five hours. But actually, the most challenging part was worrying about how to handle the simulator because we needed to know how to land and then take off on the moon.
Interviewer:	I don't think I could have coped with that!
Charles:	I'm not sure I did. But if you did something wrong, you were in trouble and we often spent eight hours a day trying to learn what to do!
Interviewer:	So how did you feel when you first heard that you were actually going to the moon?
Charles:	I suppose you're expecting me to say 'exhilarated'. But I knew there were lots of 'ifs' – it would happen if they didn't cancel the programme, if I didn't get sick and so on. So I stopped doing all the dangerous sports I was involved in.
Interviewer:	So you knew you had one chance and if you blew it, you wouldn't get another?
Charles:	That just about sums it up!
Interviewer:	And when you eventually got there, what impact did it have on you? Landing on the moon, I mean!
Charles:	When we saw the moon for the first time from about 1500 metres we recognised the landmarks but, as we got closer, we saw that the spot we were going to land on was very rough – big rocks and craters – so we panicked a bit. And the more we tried to manoeuvre and the closer we got, the more moon dust we blew out.
Interviewer:	But you landed safely?
Charles:	Eventually, yes. We were six hours late. So when we touched down, we erupted in enthusiasm. We shook hands and hugged each other.
Interviewer:	Not an easy feat in spacesuits.
Charles:	[*laughs*] No, indeed. But after that . . . we had to rest for a certain period . . . we got outside for the very first time.
Interviewer:	You must have been terrified.
Charles:	We had no sense of fear about stepping off the ladder onto the moon. We just jumped off and started bouncing around like lambs in a field in springtime.

Interviewer:	And when you saw the lunar landscape, did it live up to expectations?
Charles:	What struck me most, apart from its awesome attraction, was its desolation. The sky was jet black. You felt as if you could reach out and touch it. There were no stars and the sun was shining all the time.
Interviewer:	And what went through your mind at that moment?
Charles:	The fact that it was so untouched. The fact that nobody had ever been to that particular spot before kept returning. It was simply breathtaking.
Interviewer:	And do you have a favourite memory of the mission?
Charles:	Definitely. It was the thing that we did during the last moonwalk. We were about six kilometres or so from the base, and on the edge of a big crater, 100 metres deep. We had to be careful as we walked along the ridge because one slip would have been dangerous. Suddenly we saw this huge rock. It was a long way off, and there are no people or cars to judge distances or give you any sense of scale.
Interviewer:	But you managed to get down to it?
Charles:	Eventually. It was enormous. The biggest rock anybody had ever touched on the moon. I had a hammer and I hit a chunk of it – and it came off in my hand – a piece the size of a small melon.
Interviewer:	A different kind of souvenir! So do you think we should go back? What's the reason for investing all this time and money in the space race anyway?
Charles:	Oh, it's the prime place for a scientific base . . .

[pause]

tone

Now you'll hear the recording again.

[The recording is repeated.]

[pause]

That's the end of Part Three.
Now turn to Part Four.

[pause]

PART 4

Part Four

Part Four consists of two tasks. You'll hear five short extracts in which people are talking about an occasion when they came into contact with a well-known celebrity. Look at Task One. For questions 21 to 25, choose from the list A to H what each speaker says about coming into contact with a celebrity. Now look at Task Two. For questions 26 to 30, choose from the list A to H the opinion each speaker gives about the celebrity. While you listen you must complete both tasks. You now have 45 seconds to look at Part Four.

[pause]

tone

| Speaker One: | I was a hotel receptionist and Lenny Grade, the film producer, came rushing in one night to say he had a very important meeting in the morning. He was quite worked up about it and kept stressing how vital it was that he had an 8 o'clock alarm call. At the time I remember finding him quite patronising, because he felt he must keep repeating his request as if I was an idiot. I was doing an overnight shift and, to cut a long story short, I was having coffee before heading home when there was a commotion by the lift and he came sprinting past |

swearing. I looked at my watch and it was 9.15 – it had totally slipped my mind to wake him up.

[pause]

Speaker Two: I used to be a chauffeur ferrying around various stars to events. My most tense experience was the time I took Stan Lane to the première of his film. The tension began when the company gave me an address but I ended up on the other side of London, 15 minutes before I was due to pick him up. It was a complete catastrophe. I finally fetched him, then I ended up going through red lights and speeding, while he was panicking about being late and asking to be let out so he could get the tube. He went right over the top actually, as if it was the end of the world, even though I kept telling him we'd make it on time.

[pause]

Speaker Three: I served the tennis player Tina Sherwood with lots of fruit and vegetables in a shop in Wimbledon during the tennis tournament one year. The players used to come in and buy huge amounts of stuff to keep them going. She bought so much she was paying by credit card. I suppose she thought she didn't have to sign the slip because she was so famous, but I made her do it. She looked quite taken aback at the time, but after that, whenever I saw her in the street, she'd stop me to ask how I was. I could be wrong but I reckon she realised that, no matter how famous you are, there are still rules that apply to everyone.

[pause]

Speaker Four: I was the manager of a nightclub and one night this enormous car drew up outside the club with an extremely famous rock star in the back. His two bodyguards came up to the door and asked if they could come in and look around. I let them in, they checked out the club and reported back to him in the car. Then he came over and said that he would like to come in and could I arrange to have a special area cleared for him? As if . . . I mean, what made him think he could go to a crowded place like that and be kept apart from everyone else?

[pause]

Speaker Five: I served champagne and dinner at the film star Lena Leonard's flat once. It was a party for close family and friends and she came to the door wearing no make-up, then disappeared for two hours while we got things ready and came back into the kitchen looking a million dollars. I wandered around her flat pouring champagne for her and her guests. She gave me a very generous tip afterwards, which came as a bit of a shock because every other time I'd waited on stars they'd turned out to be rather mean. She was quite ordinary – for such a mega-star – and she didn't seem to feel she had to put on an act or anything, she was just being herself, I guess.

[pause]

tone

Now you'll hear the recording again.

[The recording is repeated.]

[pause]

That's the end of Part Four.

*There'll now be a pause of **five minutes** for you to **copy your answers onto the separate answer sheet**. Be sure to follow the numbering of all the questions. I'll remind you when there's one minute left, so that you're sure to finish in time.*

[Teacher, pause the recording here for five minutes. Remind your students when they have one minute left.]

That's the end of the test. Please stop now. Your supervisor will now collect all the question papers and answer sheets.

Test 2 Key

Paper 1   Reading (1 hour 15 minutes)

Part 1

1 C   2 B   3 A   4 C   5 B   6 D

Part 2

7 B   8 F   9 A   10 G   11 E   12 C

Part 3

13 D   14 D   15 B   16 A   17 C   18 B   19 B

Part 4

20 C   21 B   22 A   23 E   24 C   25 B   26 A   27 E   28 B   29 A
30 D   31 B   32 D   33 B   34 C

Paper 2   Writing (1 hour 30 minutes)

Task-specific Mark Schemes

Part 1

Question 1

Content (points covered)
For Band 3 or above, the candidate's **letter** must:
• describe the club's activities
• persuade new members to join.

Organisation and cohesion
Clearly organised in paragraphs.
Article format.

Range
Language of enthusiasm.
Vocabulary related to the cinema and to socialising.

Appropriacy of register and format
Any, as long as consistent.

Target reader
Would be informed and would consider joining the club.

Part 2

Question 2

Content (points covered)
For Band 3 or above, the candidate's **proposal** must:
- nominate one person
- explain why they are important to the history of the candidate's country.

Organisation and cohesion
Organised into paragraphs with a clear conclusion.

Range
Language of description, opinion and evaluation.

Appropriacy of register and format
Any, as long as consistent.

Target reader
Would be informed.

Question 3

Content (points covered)
For Band 3 or above, the candidate's **contribution** must:
- describe origins of the festival
- describe what happens
- give their opinion of why it is still important.

Organisation and cohesion
Clearly organised into paragraphs and using linking devices.

Range
Language of explanation, description, opinion.
Vocabulary related to festivals.

Appropriacy of register and format
Any, as long as consistent.

Target reader
Would be suitably informed.

Question 4

Content (points covered)
For Band 3 or above, the candidate's **report** must:
- briefly describe ONE newspaper OR magazine
- explain what the reader could learn about the culture of the country.
NB if candidate describes TWO – refer to general mark scheme
NB acceptable for candidate to use English as 'their language'

Organisation and cohesion
Clearly organised into paragraphs.

Range
The language of recommendation, justifying and explaining.

Appropriacy of register and format
Any, as long as consistent.

Target reader
Would be informed.

Question 5 (a)

Content (points covered)
For Band 3 or above, the candidate's **review** must:
• name one character in the book and explain why the candidate found him or her the most likeable
• comment on whether the candidate would or would not recommend *Lucky Jim* to other students.

Organisation and cohesion
Clearly organised into paragraphs with appropriate linking devices.

Range
Language of description, opinion and explanation.
Vocabulary related to description of character and comment on a book.

Appropriacy of register and format
Generally consistent but may mix registers if appropriate to approach taken by candidate.

Target reader
Would be informed both about the chosen character and the candidate's opinion of him or her.

Question 5 (b)

Content (points covered)
For Band 3 or above, the candidate's **essay** must:
• briefly outline the plot
• explain why the story is called *The Pelican Brief*
• say whether the candidate enjoyed the story or not.

Organisation and cohesion
Clearly organised into paragraphs with appropriate linking devices.

Range
Language of narration, explanation and opinion.
Vocabulary related to the plot of *The Pelican Brief*.

Appropriacy of register and format
Formal to unmarked. Must be consistent.

Target reader
Would be informed both about *The Pelican Brief* and about the candidate's opinion of it.

Paper 3   Use of English (1 hour)

Part 1

1 D   2 A   3 B   4 C   5 B   6 A   7 D   8 A   9 A   10 D   11 B
12 D

Part 2

13 so   14 would   15 were   16 who   17 being   18 which   19 As / Since /
Because / When   20 for / behind   21 setting   22 by / in   23 but / although   24 there
25 with   26 to   27 most / more

Part 3

28 invariably   29 alternatively   30 descriptive   31 absence   32 observations
33 opinionated   34 fairness   35 enthusiasm   36 unpredictable   37 irregular

Part 4

38 clear   39 judge   40 meet   41 space   42 aid

Part 5

43 there had not / hadn't been | so much   44 was a fall | in the   45 (quite) a name | for
46 be (very) grateful if | you would / could / 'd   47 does this bag | belong to you   48 was not /
wasn't | a / one single   49 great difficulty | (in) persuading   50 to have | been (anywhere)

Paper 4   Listening (approximately 40 minutes)

Part 1

1 A   2 B   3 A   4 A   5 B   6 C

Part 2

7 Cultural Society   8 natural science   9 butterflies, birds (in either order)   10 Let's Interact
11 German artists   12 heating   13 intimidating   14 tail

Part 3

15 C   16 B   17 D   18 C   19 A   20 C

Part 4

21 B   22 E   23 C   24 G   25 A   26 D   27 F   28 G   29 E   30 B

Transcript

This is the Cambridge Certificate in Advanced English, Listening Test. Test Two.

I'm going to give you the instructions for this test. I'll introduce each part of the test and give you time to look at the questions.

At the start of each piece you'll hear this sound:

tone

You'll hear each piece twice.

*Remember, while you're listening, write your answers on the **question paper**. You'll have **five minutes** at the end of the test to **copy your answers onto the separate answer sheet**.*

There'll now be a pause. Please ask any questions now, because you must not speak during the test.

[pause]

PART 1   *Now open your question paper and look at Part One.*

[pause]

You'll hear three different extracts. For questions one to six, choose the answer (A, B or C) which fits best according to what you hear. There are two questions for each extract.

Extract 1   *You overhear two friends, John and Diane, discussing holiday plans. Now look at questions one and two.*

[pause]

tone

John: So, Diane, have you finally decided to come to Hong Kong with us for a holiday? Your flight's reserved, we need to confirm by Wednesday.

Diane: Well, John, I've given it some thought and it's pretty tempting, but it's not that long since I last had a break. I don't know – I still haven't come to any definite decision.

John: Oh, come on, what's the problem? I know it may seem extravagant, but you told me you'd just been given promotion and a rise, so that can't be an issue, surely.

Diane: Well, it's not so much that as my work situation. Taking another break so soon after my promotion might send out the wrong message to my team, although I think my line manager would understand.

John: Of course – she knows you're a good worker.

Diane: Mmm. Well, I guess I could empty my in-tray in time – my workload's not too heavy just now. It's just that I haven't had much time to get the office organised, and to be honest, one of my colleagues would probably be only too glad to use my absence to further his own position.

John: Hmmm, sounds pretty nasty to me. Are you sure you want to carry on working there?

[pause]

tone

Now you'll hear the recording again.

[The recording is repeated.]

[pause]

Extract 2   *You overhear two friends discussing a new film. Now look at questions three and four.*

[pause]

tone

Man: I hear Joe Schultz's new film *The System* isn't going to be given the '12' certificate he wanted.

Woman: So youngsters can't see it? I'm not surprised. The reviewers say that watching the first few minutes is pretty unpleasant – there's a lot of aggression.

Man: That didn't seem to worry the authorities. Nor did the strong language, although there's quite a bit of that, but they couldn't take the little bursts of rather tense music – makes your hair stand on end, apparently!

Woman:	Interesting. Anyway, I don't think the storyline's really suitable for young children – too much delving into people's thoughts and motives.
Man:	True. You've read the book?
Woman:	Oh yeah. A great page-turner. I had no idea what the final outcome would be.
Man:	Oh, *I* guessed. I loved the way the author uses dialect all the way through – a bit out of the ordinary.
Woman:	Takes some getting used to, but it's decidedly different. You can't really believe the Prince is based on a real person from the past, though, can you?
Man:	I thought he did come over well, considering how little we know about people from that era.
Woman:	We'll go and see the film, won't we?
Man:	Definitely.

[pause]

tone

Now you'll hear the recording again.

[The recording is repeated.]

[pause]

Extract 3	*You hear an interview with the architect Ingrid Chapman, who is talking about an office building she has recently designed.*
	Now look at questions five and six.

[pause]

tone

Interviewer:	Ingrid Chapman, tell us about this new office block.
Ingrid:	It has enormous glass walls, because transparency was paramount in the brief I received from my clients – that gives it an airy, spacious feel inside. The three floors all open onto a cavernous central hall, and this is what's crucial for me – there are so many reasons for people to meet there: have a coffee, gossip, discuss formal matters in an informal setting. I force them to do these things by locating most of the services they need in this area – toilets, photocopying, café, etcetera.
Interviewer:	Forgive me, but there'll be company executives listening who are saying, 'That's all very well if you're able to design a brand new building from scratch.' What would you say to *them*?
Ingrid:	Commission me to come up with a scheme for a replacement, for example? No, seriously, it doesn't require much, a little creativity, that's all. Under-used areas can be refurbished, art hung on the walls, that sort of thing. And a questionnaire can be sent to all personnel to get their reactions to any changes you've made. Good morale facilitates productivity.

[pause]

tone

Now you'll hear the recording again.

[The recording is repeated.]

[pause]

That's the end of Part One.
Now turn to Part Two.

[pause]

PART TWO   *Part Two*

You'll hear a guide taking a group of visitors around a museum. For questions 7 to 14, complete the sentences.

You now have 45 seconds to look at Part Two.

[pause]

tone

Museum guide: Welcome to the City Museum and Art Gallery. Before we start our tour, I'd like to give you a bit of background information about the place itself.
　　The museum was founded in 1849 as a home for the collections built up over the years by the local Cultural Society, and is one of seven museums owned by the city council. Its collections of dinosaurs and mummies are well known, and it also has one of Britain's top five exhibitions of natural science. Unfortunately, not all areas are open to the public at the moment. In the cellar storerooms, for example, there are, amongst other things, display cases full of butterflies, and many others full of birds.
　　Upstairs, there's a section designed especially for children, for those of you who are interested, where young people can dress up, draw pictures, and find out about the museum at their own pace. It's called 'Let's Interact' and there's more noise there than silence, as you might imagine. But we find this to be a successful way of attracting children to museums. Let's face it, museums in the past have been boring, rather stuffy places for children, and indeed adults, to visit.
　　The picture galleries, which we'll be visiting later, boast a fine collection of drawings, prints and woodcuts by German artists, and the art collection is arranged thematically, rather than chronologically. The themes we shall see are: colour, light, movement, signs, and symbols.
　　It's a bit cold here, I'm afraid. I do apologise for this but, I'm sorry to say, the central heating needs a million-pound refit, which the city can't afford to undertake at the moment. So, if any of you are millionaires, and feeling generous today, please see me after the tour!
　　Now, if you will just follow me to the end of the Grand Colonnade, we'll turn right into the first exhibit room on the ground floor. [pause] Now, this room houses the Rutland Dinosaur. As you can see, it's three and a half metres high and fourteen metres long, quite an intimidating sight! This Cetiosaurus, as it's called, was found in England's smallest county in 1968. The creature loped across the countryside 175 million years ago, and is the most complete example of the breed discovered to date. Most of the neck, some of the spine and a bit of the tail were found in Rutland; the rest of the tail is polystyrene. For those of you who prefer your dinosaurs on a much more human scale, there is a much smaller 200-million-year-old Pilosaur over there.

Now, if you'd like to follow me up the stairs, we'll make our way to the . . .

[pause]

tone

Now you'll hear the recording again.

[The recording is repeated.]

[pause]

That's the end of Part Two.
Now turn to Part Three.

[pause]

PART 3

Part Three

You'll hear part of a radio interview in which Harry and Jennifer, two members of an after-work adult drama class, are asked about their reasons for attending the class. For questions 15 to 20, choose the answer (A, B, C or D) which fits best according to what you hear. You now have one minute to look at Part Three.

[pause]

tone

Interviewer: I gather these drama courses which you are attending have really given you a new lease of life. Jennifer, can you try and explain the fascination you derive from a hard three-hour session at the college after a full day's work?

Jennifer: Above all, each session is fun, it energises me. I actually go home with more energy on a Tuesday than any other day of the week. The reason is simple, I feel alive after the drama classes. At first I wasn't sure if I would enjoy the course; you have to relate to the others in the group. In fact most of the work is in small groups or at least in pairs and obviously the natural barriers between strangers exist. I can honestly say that from the first evening this did not bother me, and I'm not an extrovert by nature. In fact, if anything, I'm rather shy and reserved.

Interviewer: And what about you, Harry?

Harry: Well, as far as I'm concerned, drama classes have freed me, they've allowed me to be creative and successful in so many ways that I'm not, usually. I particularly enjoy the sessions when we just create something out of nothing, we improvise. There is usually some time in the evening when we make up either a character or a conversation or a situation and act that out with the others. The spontaneous nature of improvisation is what's so appealing to me.

Jennifer: You can't 'get it wrong', you're having a go, that's all. I mean you just stand up and become another person for five minutes; perhaps you're like yourself or totally different, that doesn't matter. What counts is that you take on a new personality, and you actually become that person. And, since you invent the part, you can't be out of character and it's impossible to make mistakes. I expect this will change when we move onto text, won't it, Harry?

Harry: Yes, yes, I'm really looking forward to using text in the classes and even to learning lines. I just find some text fascinating and can't wait to really work on it. Of course it will be different from improvisation, where we make up the parts we play, but I know you can lose yourself in a part, and playing it your way is going to be the challenge.

Jennifer: Obviously, a specific part will be open to interpretation and a director may want you to do it in a certain way. Imagine playing a Shakespearean hero or heroine, well, there are bound to be different ways of saying those famous lines and the actor or actress may not agree with the director, but this is a stage we haven't reached yet. For the moment, it's about overcoming self-consciousness and learning to be sensitive. Last week we had a new person in the group and it became really clear that he hadn't tuned in to the way in which the classes work, you know, it was embarrassing really, he overdid it and tried to dominate the group, he didn't wait and watch and listen. This was when it struck me that we've been learning to listen to each other and to respond accordingly; and of course you bring yourself into it, but not too much and not too inappropriately.

Harry: I couldn't agree more. He actually asked me personal questions which were intrusive and could have been saved for the tea break. I found it off the point and distracting. Well, I suppose he felt awkward too, but if I've learned anything this term, it's not to jump in, but to take my time and allow the others time by being patient when they are struggling with, for example, creating an unfamiliar character. The group has to develop together and the newcomer was an outsider. I guess it wasn't his fault, but he didn't seem interested in learning from the situation. That's probably what annoyed me.

Jennifer: I'd be surprised if he came again. He didn't look comfortable.

Interviewer: Would you say this receptiveness to each other is the key lesson so far, Jennifer?

[pause]

tone

Now you'll hear the recording again.

[The recording is repeated.]

[pause]

That's the end of Part Three.
Now turn to Part Four.

[pause]

PART 4

Part Four

Part Four consists of two tasks. You will hear five short extracts in which British people are talking about living abroad. Look at Task One. For questions 21 to 25, choose from the list A to H each speaker's present occupation. Now look at Task Two. For questions 26 to 30, choose from the list A to H the main advantage each speaker mentions about living where they do. While you listen you must complete both tasks. You now have 45 seconds to look at Part Four.

[pause]

tone

[pause]

Speaker One: I'd often thought about living here, but my husband's work as Head of Personnel for an engineering firm tied him to the UK and I worked in a hospital. Of course, we came here on holiday and got to know the place. Now we've retired here, we don't have to go home at the end of the summer and face the harsh English winter, and that's the greatest bonus without a doubt. We're getting used to the local people. They try to help us, though we're not proficient in the language yet. It's not hard picking it up in shops and cafes, and of course there's TV too.

[pause]

Speaker Two: I was posted here three years ago. At first, I wasn't very keen on the idea of coming. It's hardly a very cultural place, is it? But frankly it's grown on me. I'm quite an outdoor person too and what I really appreciate are the many leisure opportunities and people with time on their hands to share them with. Obviously, the weather helps, although it's unbearably hot in July. The embassy pool and squash courts are quite reasonable and we have access to other facilities locally. There are a few tournaments during the year – not very high standard but quite fun. I've also taken up a new interest – old buildings. The local architecture's fascinating!

[pause]

Speaker Three: I'd always intended to travel, do a few short contracts in faraway places and then go home to study to be a specialist. So I came here 20 years ago and . . . sort of stayed. Initially, the work was quite different from what I dealt with in my surgery in London, although it's routine now. It's certainly a good lifestyle, I have to admit, very reasonable remuneration for the hours I have to put in, and that's the key. It allows me to put something by for my retirement and indulge my hobbies. It's a good place to grow old – sports, great golf courses for example, if you're interested, which I'm not really! (laughs).

[pause]

Speaker Four: I started work near London, doing a very routine job, maintaining equipment in a water purification plant. Then I was asked to come out here. I wasn't keen at first as it involved working in the mountains on a new dam. I decided to try it for a year because the salary was acceptable and I thought the experience would be useful. But I stayed on because the job provides so much variety. I head a team of workers now on a new project, things I wouldn't normally get to do at my age. I live in a basic bungalow with amazing views over the plantations and rice fields. It's great!

[pause]

Speaker Five: It all started when I came here on holiday. I was wandering around the market, looking for souvenirs and the craftsmanship impressed me. They're great at carving wood or weaving fabrics. I'd been thinking of taking early retirement, then it struck me. Why not set up something of my own here? So I began in a small way, sending local handicrafts and produce back to small specialist shops. It took off and now I supply large department stores. It's hard, working for yourself, but I love being here because the locals are so easy to get on with. They'll always give you a helping hand and I feel part of things, which is great . . .

[pause]

tone

Now you'll hear the recording again.

[The recording is repeated.]

[pause]

That's the end of Part Four.
*There'll now be a pause of **five minutes** for you to **copy your answers onto the separate answer sheet**. Be sure to follow the numbering of all the questions. I'll remind you when there's one minute left, so that you're sure to finish in time.*

[Teacher, pause the recording here for five minutes. Remind your students when they have one minute left.]

That's the end of the test. Please stop now. Your supervisor will now collect all the question papers and answer sheets.

Test 3 Key

Paper 1   Reading (1 hour 15 minutes)

Part 1
1 B   2 A   3 B   4 A   5 D   6 B

Part 2
7 D   8 B   9 A   10 F   11 G   12 C

Part 3
13 C   14 A   15 D   16 B   17 B   18 D   19 A

Part 4
20 C   21 E   22 D   23 C   24 D   25 E   26 B   27 A   28 B   29 D
30 A   31 B   32 C   33 D   34 A

Paper 2   Writing (1 hour 30 minutes)

Task-specific Mark Schemes

Part 1

Question 1

Content (points covered)
For Band 3 or above, the candidate's **report** must:
- make recommendations
- justify choices.

Organisation and cohesion
Clearly organised report, possibly with headings.

Range
Language of description, explanation, justification.

Appropriacy of register and format
Any, as long as appropriate and consistent.

Target reader
Would be informed.

Part 2

Question 2

Content (points covered)
For Band 3 or above, the candidate's **article** must:
- state whether there should be more or less tourism in region
- describe benefits of existing tourist activity in region
- describe possible disadvantages of increased tourism.

Organisation and cohesion
Clearly organised in paragraphs.

Range
Language of description and opinion. Vocabulary related to tourism.

Appropriacy of register and format
Any, as long as consistent.

Target reader
Would be informed and consider publishing the article.

Question 3

Content (points covered)
For Band 3 or above, the candidate's **competition entry** must:
• describe what teacher taught him/her
• explain how teacher influenced him/her
• justify teacher's nomination for award.

Organisation and cohesion
Clearly paragraphed.

Range
Language of description, evaluation and justification.
Vocabulary related to teaching/learning.

Appropriacy of register and format
Any. May mix registers if appropriate to approach taken by candidate.

Target reader
Would be informed.

Question 4

Content (points covered)
For Band 3 or above, the candidate's **review** must:
• specify and describe two websites
• assess the user-friendliness of the sites
• explain why these sites are useful for students.

Organisation and cohesion
Clear organisation with appropriate paragraphing. (NB letter format is acceptable.)

Range
Language of description, evaluation and comparison/contrast.
Vocabulary related to studying and websites.

Appropriacy of register and format
Any, as long as consistent.

Target reader
Would be informed.

Question 5 (a)

Content (points covered)
For Band 3 or above, the candidate's **article** must:
• recommend *Lucky Jim* as a good story for a film
• explain why the candidate thinks it would make a good film.

Organisation and cohesion
Clearly organised into paragraphs with appropriate linking devices.

Range
Language of description, opinion and explanation.
Vocabulary related to stories and films.

Appropriacy of register and format
Generally consistent but may mix registers if appropriate to approach taken by candidate.

Target reader
Would be informed and would be persuaded that *Lucky Jim* might make a successful film.

Question 5 (b)

Content (points covered)
For Band 3 or above, the candidate's **essay** must:
• outline the role of politics in *The Pelican Brief*
• comment on whether the candidate feels such events could happen in real life.

Organisation and cohesion
Clearly organised into paragraphs with appropriate linking devices.

Range
Language of narration, evaluation and opinion.
Vocabulary related to the plot of *The Pelican Brief* and to opinions of events in the story.

Appropriacy of register and format
Consistently formal to unmarked.

Target reader
Would be informed both about the role of politics in *The Pelican Brief* and about the candidate's opinion as to the realism of such events.

Paper 3   Use of English (1 hour)

Part 1

1 C   2 D   3 C   4 A   5 A   6 B   7 C   8 D   9 B   10 C   11 D
12 D

Part 2

13 as   14 every / any   15 for / by / from / through   16 who / that   17 over   18 to
19 yet / but / although / though NOT while   20 in   21 are   22 what   23 How
24 than   25 whether / either   26 your / an   27 which

Part 3

28 kingdom   29 unspoilt / unspoiled   30 enthusiasts   31 practical   32 colourful / colorful   33 hazardous   34 undertake   35 unfortunately   36 sustainability
37 requirements

Part 4

38 operate   39 point   40 material   41 released   42 make

Part 5

43 account should | this / the door be (kept)   **44** condition | (that) it is hard to   **45** far as | punctuality is concerned   **46** for a great / good deal | of patience   **47** was only | when / after   **48** no support | from   **49** (of things) to offer | in   **50** prevent it | (from) becoming / being OR prevent its | becoming / being

Paper 4   **Listening** (approximately 40 minutes)

Part 1

1 A   **2** C   **3** A   **4** B   **5** A   **6** C

Part 2

7 envelope   **8** fort   **9** legal   **10** transportation   **11** computer vision   **12** wax
13 laser   **14** ink

Part 3

15 B   **16** C   **17** A   **18** D   **19** C   **20** B

Part 4

21 B   **22** F   **23** D   **24** H   **25** C   **26** G   **27** A   **28** H   **29** E   **30** D

Transcript	*This is the Cambridge Certificate in Advanced English Listening Test. Test Three. I'm going to give you the instructions for this test. I'll introduce each part of the test and give you time to look at the questions.*
	At the start of each piece you'll hear this sound:
	tone
	You'll hear each piece twice.
	*Remember, while you're listening, write your answers on the **question paper**. You'll have **five minutes** at the end of the test to **copy your answers onto the separate answer sheet**.*
	There'll now be a pause. Please ask any questions now, because you must not speak during the test.
	[pause]
PART 1	*Now open your question paper and look at Part One.*
	[pause]
	You'll hear three different extracts. For questions one to six, choose the answer (A, B or C) which fits best according to what you hear. There are two questions for each extract.
Extract 1	*You hear two colleagues, Eva and Colin, talking about a problem at work. Now look at questions one and two.*

[pause]

tone

Eva: So the thing is, you aren't getting on with our new boss then, Colin?

Colin: She's just so different from her predecessor. I mean, *John* used to get us *all* involved in the decision-making process.

Eva: No chance of that with Sandra, you think?

Colin: No way! OK, I grant you, she's got some good ideas – she moved pretty fast to get us all to agree to individual job descriptions and a proper timetable, none of which we've had before and we should have had. And she's done her homework on the staff profile, our qualifications and past experience and so on . . .

Eva: As you'd expect.

Colin: Yes. But she doesn't seem aware of the atmosphere here – it's the way we've always done things. I just don't feel I can work with her.

Eva: I'd say she's just finding her feet in a new job, and she'll soon get the hang of what we're all about. Let's focus on how much she's already achieved. I wouldn't let anybody tell you it's a trivial issue, though. If she doesn't settle in soon, and you still have issues with her, I think you should approach her direct.

Colin: OK, thanks, Eva.

[pause]

tone

Now you'll hear the recording again.

[The recording is repeated.]

[pause]

Extract 2 *You hear an interview with an expert who repairs antique vases. Now look at questions three and four.*

[pause]

tone

Interviewer: Show me how you do it. I see you've got trays and trays of pieces here.

Expert: Yes, you have to find the bits that match, so I've put all these tiny pieces into colour groups – red here, blue over there. It's a bit like doing a jigsaw, really. But at least there are no stains to remove. All we have to be aware of is the enamel on the surface; that we have to lift all the dirt and grease off. If you don't, the pieces won't go back together again, it'll fall apart. If the cracks are going to show, they've got to be really clean, otherwise they'll look messy.

Interviewer: You want the cracks to show? Some people would say that's terrible, for such a valuable vase.

Expert: Well, yes, they probably would, but something that's broken so extensively as this, if you cover all the cracks up you're really making a fake. Being broken is something that's happened to it in its lifetime, which should be recorded, and as long as you can restore it so that aesthetically it still works, it shouldn't matter that the cracks show . . .

[pause]

tone

Now you'll hear the recording again.

[The recording is repeated.]

[pause]

| Extract 3 | | *On the radio, you hear a visitor talking to a man about the remote island where he lives. Now look at questions five and six.* |

[pause]

tone

Woman:	This is such an unusual place because there's no public transport to the island – I came here in your fishing boat. The result is a paradise – rich marine life, unspoilt countryside. Yet you want to let the world in – you've campaigned to start up a ferry service from the mainland. Why?
Man:	There isn't enough work to support our population. If visitors come to the island – and we have a lot to offer them – catering for them would create employment. Also our young people would be able to commute to jobs on the mainland.
Woman:	Don't you think it's risky? These beaches could be covered with holiday houses and hotels; your visitors will complain because there are only a few shops. And a ferry service won't be enough. People will want to fly here, and you'll have to build an airport. No more paradise!
Man:	We can build a small airport without impacting on our quality of life here, and it makes economic sense. Our shops can cope with more people on the island – it'll be seasonal anyway. And why would we build on the beaches? It'd be crazy.
Woman:	I hope you're right.

[pause]

tone

Now you'll hear the recording again.

[The recording is repeated.]

[pause]

That's the end of Part One.
Now turn to Part Two.

[pause]

PART 2   *Part Two*

You'll hear a short radio report about how technology is helping archaeologists who want to learn more about some texts written over 2,000 years ago known as Roman tablets. For questions 7 to 14, complete the sentences. You now have 45 seconds to look at Part Two.

[pause]

tone

Man: At the time of the Roman Empire in Europe, around 2,000 years ago, it was common for information to be written, not on paper, but on things called 'tablets'. These were pieces of wood about the size and thickness of a typical modern envelope.

Hundreds of such tablets have been unearthed from archaeological sites throughout Europe and the Mediterranean world – nearly 200 were found in one Roman fort alone – and like most of these discoveries, they have been placed in public collections, mainly in museums in northern Europe, to be viewed but not, unfortunately, to be read.

This is because, although in some cases traces of writing can still be seen, most are now illegible to the naked eye. But that's all soon to change because archaeologists hope that with the help of new technology, their secrets may soon be revealed. Many of the tablets took the form of legal documents and letters written by Roman soldiers. An example, now at the British Museum, bears the name of the person who wrote it and the name of the person who received it, plus the word 'transportation', which you can just make out, but the rest remains a mystery. Now, with the help of computer techniques, experts hope eventually to be able to read the whole letter. Professor Mike Brady, a leading figure in what's known as 'computer vision' for many years, admits that this is the hardest project he's ever worked on. But the excitement of seeing the latest ideas in computing applied to such a very ancient problem has the archaeological community buzzing.

So, in simple terms, why has the writing been preserved and how will it be possible to 'undo' the ageing process? Well, the tablets were made with thin, hollow panels cut across them. Wax was poured into these and the text was then written into this soft surface using an instrument with a fine metal point. In virtually all cases, the wax has perished and all that can be detected on the surface of the tablet underneath are scratches. These are too faint to be read, because they are distorted.

For some time, scientists have attempted to study them with laser photography, but this has proved fruitless. However, it is now hoped that by enhancing images of the tablets on computer, their original messages will become legible again. If this is the case, a whole new source of historical information will be opened up, and this promises advances and new knowledge for many decades to come. The new technology has already been used on texts in ink as well, and in the future, it will be applied to damaged surfaces of many kinds.

[pause]

tone

Now you'll hear the recording again.

[The recording is repeated.]

[pause]

That's the end of Part Two.
Now turn to Part Three.

[pause]

PART 3   *Part Three*

You'll hear an interview with an architect called Lucy Collett who designs small buildings. For questions 15 to 20, choose the answer (A, B, C or D) which fits best according to what you hear. You now have one minute to look at Part Three.

[pause]

tone

Interviewer: I'm sitting here, rather uncomfortably, with designer Lucy Collett. Lucy, you're an architect really, but an architect with a difference.

Lucy Collett: Yes, I specialise in small buildings.

Interviewer: And we're in one of your buildings now. It's a tree-house, and we're perched on child-size seats, two or three metres above the ground.

Lucy Collett: In fact, I was commissioned to design this house by my neighbours for their children. I don't like heights, but I loved the challenge of weaving the house in amongst the branches. You can see there are several storeys with stairways between them.

Interviewer: I'd have given anything for a house like this when I was a child. What started you off on this type of design?

Lucy Collett: I've always had a passion for small buildings. Play houses, of course, when I was a little girl. Then I found a book about historical telephone boxes, which fascinated me. When the telephone was an amazing new invention, money was poured into the designs of public phone boxes. They were all sizes and styles. There were some that looked like rustic cottages, with thatched roofs; others like Chinese pagodas; one like a sort of Greek temple. Some were quite luxurious, with chairs, and people used to go in there to play cards. But it didn't last long; they had to be standardised and made more practical.

Interviewer: You went to architecture school. Did you know you were going to work on this small scale?

Lucy Collett: Yes, my final year project was on small buildings in an industrial context. If you look at major building sites, they're dotted around with huts and temporary buildings. You think, 'They put up these tin boxes for the workers to drink their tea and read their newspapers in. What is there to that?' Well, they've all got to conform to safety standards, and why shouldn't they have some style as well? I designed them to look better, and also to be put up and dismantled more quickly. I worked on durability of materials, comfort and so on.

Interviewer: Where did you get your inventiveness from?

Lucy Collett: I don't know. I think I'm more practical than inventive. My parents were market stall holders. They had a really cumbersome stall which took them forever to put up. All the market people started setting up about four o'clock in the morning. It was freezing, back-breaking work, and it drove me mad when I had to help them. I was visiting some clients abroad a few years ago, and saw some brilliant stalls in their local market. They were little metal folding houses, completely waterproof and enclosed, with plenty of display room. At the end of the day you could lock them up with the goods safe inside, or you could fold them flat and cart them off to the next town. I did drawings of them and made one when I got home. But I haven't sold it.

Interviewer: What have you done that you're most proud of?

Lucy Collett: I suppose everything I've done is a variation on a theme, so it's hard to pick anything out. But I did get an award. The Newspaper Sellers' Association gave me a prize for a design I did for street corner kiosks – you know, those cute little buildings with display windows on three sides. Mine were in strong steel, painted, with domed roofs and lots of decorative detail. I must admit, I was particularly pleased with the fancy work, and the newspaper people loved it.

Interviewer: Have you ever done any phone box designs, since that was what started you off?

Lucy Collett: Funnily enough, that's what I've just been doing. For an international hotel chain. They'd stopped putting public phone booths in their hotel lobbies because of mobile phones, but there were complaints from a few countries where mobiles hadn't really caught on yet. So the hotel decided to make a big feature of lobby phone boxes. I did these sort of glass bird-cage designs, with brass work and over-the-top telephones. Now the company's putting them in all their hotels, and people are going into them to make calls on their mobiles. It's sort of retro-style lobby furniture.

Interviewer: And tree-houses?

Lucy Collett: No, this is a one-off. I've told you, I'm scared of heights.

Interviewer: Okay. Shall we let down the ladder and go home? Thank you, Lucy.

[pause]

tone

Now you'll hear the recording again.

[The recording is repeated.]

[pause]

That's the end of Part Three.
Now turn to Part Four.

[pause]

PART 4

Part Four

Part Four consists of two tasks. you'll hear five short extracts in which people are talking about problems related to their work. Look at Task One. For questions 21 to 25, choose from the list A to H the problem each person encounters. Now look at Task Two. For questions 26 to 30, choose from the list A to H each person's current feeling. While you listen you must complete both tasks. You now have 45 seconds to look at Part Four.

[pause]

tone

Speaker One: The weird thing is, that up to quite recently, I used to really love being in the theatre business, so it never seemed much of a hardship earning next to nothing and holding meetings in an office the size of a shoebox. But somehow, over the past year, the gloss seems to have worn off a bit. And now I've realised I'm just being taken for granted, I feel as though my spirit's been broken – it's awful. I don't blame anyone for it – we've had no actual rows – but I won't put up with it. It won't be easy, entering the job market all over again, though.

[pause]

Speaker Two: Normally I'd say I thrive on deadlines and pressure from clients, but it does all build up, and recently I've been prone to fairly severe headaches in the office. Don't get me wrong – I'm fine outside work – I can chill out with the best of them. But I do have a lot on my plate, as you'd expect at my level in the company, and it's probably too much to handle, if I'm honest, especially with my current project. I can't wait to see what happens when I implement my new time-management plan at work. It's hardly rocket science, but I'll be devastated if it doesn't work.

[pause]

Speaker Three: The thing that finally made me flip was being told to move into a new office which was patently unsuitable for the project I was working on. That was on top of a whole series of other ridiculous demands. So the trouble was, it just all came to a head, and the people in charge simply refused to take responsibility for it. We had a number of bitter exchanges, and I ended up seething with rage. I still feel that way. But I'm determined not to just accept it, although I have no idea what I should do about it. It all happened so fast! You can bet I won't be leaving though because I love the work.

[pause]

Speaker Four: I'm rapidly reaching the end of my tether. I haven't lost my cool with a customer yet but it'll happen soon! It's just too much, being expected to run my department without a reliable flow of data. My line manager's been very supportive, I'll give her that, and she's been on at the technicians to sort it out. So I've done my bit, but nothing's happened yet. And the final straw is when I'm deluged with supposedly helpful emails from other departmental heads, about how to cope! What do *they* know about it? They go on and on about how disastrous it is, as if it's my fault! Luckily I've got a great team under me.

[pause]

Speaker Five: Well, I'm not sure what my options are. She's got such a bee in her bonnet about this internal promotion that you just can't reason with her, so I haven't tried to talk her out of it. I really don't want to get her into trouble by reporting her to management for that row yesterday – it would ruin morale in the office. I suppose in the end we might *both* get a small pay rise and a new job title. If she isn't satisfied with that, and I have a feeling she won't be, I'll have to raise the whole issue with the boss, and let him resolve it.

[pause]

tone

Now you'll hear the recording again.

[The recording is repeated.]

[pause]

That's the end of Part Four.
*There'll now be a pause of **five minutes** for you to **copy your answers onto the separate answer sheet**. Be sure to follow the numbering of all the questions. I'll remind you when there's one minute left, so that you're sure to finish in time.*

[Teacher, pause the recording here for five minutes. Remind your students when they have one minute left.]

That's the end of the test. Please stop now. Your supervisor will now collect all the question papers and answer sheets.

Test 4 Key

Paper 1   Reading (1 hour 15 minutes)

Part 1

1 B   2 D   3 B   4 C   5 D   6 D

Part 2

7 D   8 B   9 G   10 C   11 A   12 F

Part 3

13 B   14 A   15 C   16 A   17 B   18 A   19 D

Part 4

20 D   21 B   22 D   23 C   24 A   25 B   26 C   27 D   28 A   29 D
30 B   31 A   32 C   33 D   34 B

Paper 2   Writing (1 hour 30 minutes)

Task-specific Mark Schemes

Part 1

Question 1

Content (points covered)
For Band 3 or above, the candidate's **proposal** must:
• explain why improvements are necessary
• outline how facilities could be improved
(more able candidates will focus more effectively on target reader's requirements).

Organisation and cohesion
Clearly organised into paragraphs with suitable linking devices.
Headed sections may be an advantage.

Range
Language of explanation and suggestion.
Vocabulary related to learning facilities.

Appropriacy of register and format
Formal to unmarked.

Target reader
Would be informed.

Part 2

Question 2

Content (points covered)
For Band 3 or above, the candidate's **article** must:

- discuss advantages and/or disadvantages of increased use of technology in field of communication
- give reasons for views.

Organisation and cohesion
Clearly organised in paragraphs.

Range
Language of opinion.
Vocabulary related to technology and communications.

Appropriacy of register and format
Any, may mix registers if appropriate to approach taken by candidate.

Target reader
Would be informed.

Question 3

Content (points covered)
For Band 3 or above, the candidate's **contribution** must:
- describe how important public transport is in his/her country
- explain why people are willing/unwilling to use it
- suggest ways public transport could be improved.

Organisation and cohesion
Clearly organised in paragraphs.
Headings appropriate.

Range
Transport-related vocabulary.
Language of description, explanation and suggestion.

Appropriacy of register and format
Formal to unmarked.

Target reader
Would be informed.

Question 4

Content (points covered)
For Band 3 or above, the candidate's **letter of application** must:
- explain why they want to participate
- explain why they should be chosen with reference to skills and personality.

Organisation and cohesion
Clearly organised in paragraphs with appropriate linking.

Range
Vocabulary related to character.
Language of persuasion.

Appropriacy of register and format
Any, as long as consistent.

Target reader
Would be informed and consider the candidate's application.

Question 5 (a)

Content (points covered)
For Band 3 or above, the candidate's **essay** must:

- discuss how Jim's attitude to work influences his actions
- say whether the candidate does or does not sympathise with his actions.

Organisation and cohesion
Clearly organised into paragraphs with appropriate linking devices.

Range
Language of description, evaluation and opinion.
Vocabulary related to attitudes towards work.

Appropriacy of register and format
Formal to unmarked.
Must be consistent.

Target reader
Would be informed both about Jim and about the candidate's opinion of him.

Question 5 (b)

Content (points covered)
For Band 3 or above, the candidate's **article** must:
- describe the role played by the 'bad guys' in *The Pelican Brief*
- comment on how the candidate feels they add to the excitement of the plot.

Organisation and cohesion
Clearly organised into paragraphs with appropriate linking devices.

Range
Language of narration, evaluation and opinion.
Vocabulary related to the plot of *The Pelican Brief* and to commenting on a story.

Appropriacy of register and format
May mix registers if appropriate to approach taken by candidate.

Target reader
Would be informed both about the book and about the candidate's opinions of the role of the 'bad guys'.

Paper 3   Use of English (1 hour)

Part 1

1 B   2 D   3 C   4 A   5 B   6 A   7 A   8 B   9 A   10 C   11 B
12 C

Part 2

13 which   14 that   15 not / hardly   16 its   17 would / could   18 on
19 however / though   20 one   21 to   22 At / In   23 like   24 with / having
25 a   26 less   27 because

Part 3

28 existence   29 civilisations / civilizations   30 reliably   31 performer(s)   32 variety
33 increasingly   34 standardized / standardised   35 addition   36 significantly
37 intensity

Part 4

38 field   39 held   40 felt   41 change   42 dropped

Part 5

43 on the point | of leaving   44 to work as | a volunteer   45 is / has been scheduled | to take
46 you notify us | of any   47 lack / absence of (any) | leadership that caused   48 of her | decision
to   49 cut down (on) | the amount / quantity   50 no / little time | (in) starting / getting started

Paper 4   Listening (approximately 40 minutes)

Part 1

1 A   2 B   3 B   4 C   5 C   6 B

Part 2

7 apples   8 (plastic) tunnel   9 wax   10 balloon   11 green
12 12 years / twelve years   13 Sweetheart   14 (cherry) stone

Part 3

15 D   16 A   17 C   18 C   19 D   20 C

Part 4

21 H   22 C   23 D   24 E   25 G   26 E   27 D   28 G   29 C   30 A

Transcript

This is the Cambridge Certificate in Advanced English, Listening Test. Test Four. I'm going to give you the instructions for this test.
I'll introduce each part of the test and give you time to look at the questions.

At the start of each piece you'll hear this sound:

tone

You'll hear each piece twice.

*Remember, while you're listening, write your answers on the **question paper**. You'll have five minutes at the end of the test to **copy your answers onto the separate answer sheet**.*

There'll now be a pause. Please ask any questions now, because you must not speak during the test.

[pause]

PART 1

Now open your question paper and look at Part One.

[pause]

You'll hear three different extracts. For questions one to six, choose the answer (A, B or C) which fits best according to what you hear. There are two questions for each extract.

Extract 1

You hear part of a radio discussion about a football team. Now look at questions one and two.

[pause]

tone

Woman:	So is John Elliott a player you like to watch? I'm guessing he is.
Man:	Yes, he's excellent, very technical, clever with the ball; he's good at passing the ball to the team's top goal scorers and setting them up to shoot. When he sees that final pass coming as he approaches the goal area, you get a lot of players who get there but then freeze and get erratic, but he's not one of them. So if you can get him backing up the strikers, he can be the key player.
Woman:	And what about their new man, Danny Martinez? Seven million they paid for him, they've probably overpaid. Not very cautious given that they've paid out this kind of cash before and it all went wrong, didn't it? They'll want to hang on to him come what may, at that price . . .
Man:	Yes, well, it hasn't broken the bank, but they were overcharged for him. They probably thought he was a good investment – he's young, they can sell him on if things go wrong, for more money. They got their fingers burnt once over a similar deal, and they won't want it to happen again.

[pause]

tone

Now you'll hear the recording again.

[The recording is repeated.]

[pause]

Extract 2

You hear part of a radio interview with Deanna Carriconde, who has just won a prize for her environmental work in South America. Now look at questions three and four.

[pause]

tone

Interviewer:	Congratulations, Deanna!
Deanna:	Thanks very much.
Interviewer:	Were you surprised to win?
Deanna:	Completely!
Interviewer:	Now you're trying to save a wildlife habitat that stretches 3,000 kilometres along the coast of South America. Aren't you daunted by that?
Deanna:	It's a huge task but we're basically getting the message out: the local fish population – mainly anchovies – are being forced into colder water because the sea's warming up. Of those left, 85 per cent are being scooped up by industrial fishing trawlers so predators like seals, penguins and dolphins – and local fishermen – are left with very little. Now this is the richest ecosystem in the world. If it's starting to be affected, you know there must be a tremendous impact on other less robust systems.
Interviewer:	So what's your relationship like with local fishermen?
Deanna:	They used to regard me as an enemy because I used to work for seals, and as you know, fishermen and seals compete for the same fish – but now they see me as an ally trying to control industrial fishing.
Interviewer:	What – stopping them scooping up anchovies?
Deanna:	Not stopping them, but getting them to catch less; which means the local fishermen can catch more of the large fish that feed on the anchovies.

[pause]

tone

Now you'll hear the recording again.

[The recording is repeated.]

[pause]

Extract 3

You hear part of a radio programme about books and reading. Now look at questions five and six.

[pause]

tone

Neil: Today we're talking about books that have inspired us, books that have made a difference to our lives. Each of my studio guests has chosen what for them was an important book and first off we're going to hear about Monica Nairn's choice. Monica.

Monica: Thanks, Neil. Well the thing about this book is that when I first discovered it in my late teens – it was a birthday present, if I remember correctly – I'd never really read anything like it before. I'd heard about it from a friend, and I'd got the idea it was something special and so I asked for it specifically. I think I was about 17, so I was a fairly late developer as a reader. I hadn't been particularly interested up till then, but it suddenly sort of took a grip. I think it was the strangeness of that book; I mean it's the one I'd take with me to a desert island because it's just got everything in it and it just opened me up to what pleasures there are in description, in narrative, you know, in ideas.

Neil: Well, we'll discover exactly which book my next guest has chosen . . .

[pause]

tone

Now you'll hear the recording again.

[The recording is repeated.]

[pause]

That's the end of Part One.
Now turn to Part Two.

[pause]

PART 2

Part Two

You'll hear part of a radio programme about cherries, small fruit which grow on trees. For questions 7 to 14, complete the sentences. You now have 45 seconds to look at Part Two.

[pause]

tone

When I visited a number of fruit farms in central England, I found broad agreement among most of the growers that these days it makes sense to move away from their traditional crops such as apples and into cherries instead. Now, in summertime, they have orchard after orchard of beautiful trees, heavily laden with bright red fruit.

UK cherry growers tend to choose the varieties which ripen slowly. This fruit may command a higher price because the harvest is not so early, and there are always reliable buyers for it. Research is currently being carried out into ways of improving yield. A major obstacle to efficient production is the fact that growth may not be consistent from season to season. Sometimes the fruit only grows as big as a pea, and then drops to the ground.

Quite a few of the smaller trees are covered up against the rain and wind, in a plastic tunnel. Older, larger trees have to take their chance out in the open, but cherries are a delicate fruit, and optimum weather conditions are needed to achieve the potential yield of five tonnes per hectare. The surface of the fruit has very little wax on it, so cherries need to be kept out of the rain as much as possible, because the skin is liable to crack when water gets into it. If this occurs, the crop may be lost, because the fruit bursts with a pop, rather like a balloon.

When you're selecting the best cherries to buy, don't get them if they look at all tired or wrinkled, and buy the ones with a green stem. You'll find they taste much better than ones without.

People often ask, 'How long does it take to get a decent crop from a cherry tree?' Well, there are new varieties, laden with fruit, that are only four years old, but if you go back and read the old fruit-growing textbooks from the 1960s, they tell you cherries don't give a worthwhile crop till they're 12 years old. Some varieties go on cropping till they're 90!

There are three new varieties which have recently been introduced by growers. 'Symphony' and 'Staccato' are both highly successful so far, but 'Sweetheart' is being planted in larger numbers than either of them and looks to be a real winner.

Just one problem if you go cherry picking this summer – how do you stop yourself eating them all? One expert who's been picking all her life told me, 'Eat a cherry, suck the stone and keep it on your tongue – it stops you putting any more in!' That way you end up with at least a handful of this delicious fruit in your basket!

[pause]

tone

Now you'll hear the recording again.

[The recording is repeated.]

[pause]

That's the end of Part Two.
Now turn to Part Three.

[pause]

PART 3

Part Three

You'll hear a radio interview in which an artist called Sophie Axel is talking about her life and career. For questions 15 to 20, choose the answer (A, B, C or D) which fits best according to what you hear. You now have one minute to look at Part Three.

[pause]

tone

Interviewer:	So here we are today in the artist Sophie Axel's – em – amazingly colourful home!
Sophie:	Do you mean shockingly colourful? You don't have to be polite!
Interviewer:	Well, it was quite a surprise when you opened the front door.
Sophie:	That's how it's meant to be, really. A huge impact of colour on the senses. Electric pink, brilliant blue and yellow for the hallway – in fact all the walls in the house are different colours. It's *so* stimulating.
Interviewer:	So would you say colour is the most important thing in your life, Sophie?
Sophie:	Absolutely. It's in me. I don't pay any conscious attention to it, it's who I am, what I have grown up with. It's like an internal microchip. For me, every number and every day has a colour; when I sleep, I even dream in colour. And I associate people with colours too.
Interviewer:	I won't ask you what mine is! I noticed before that you've even got rainbow stairs.
Sophie:	Oh, the children adore them – it's their favourite place to play.
Interviewer:	They're quite small, aren't they? You're not worried about them falling?
Sophie:	No – they're as sure-footed as goats, even the baby! Life is never without danger. I just leave them to it and they develop confidence at their own rate, as children should. They need to find themselves – specially if they're going to follow the family's artistic tradition.
Interviewer:	You mean your family are artists too?
Sophie:	Not as such, but we're all very creative, specially the female side of the family. My grandmother was an actress – she's still alive; and my mother and aunt are furniture designers – for quite famous international companies actually.
Interviewer:	So when you get together . . .
Sophie:	Oh, there's no stopping us! We're all very expressive in words, in clothes, in the environment we create in our homes.
Interviewer:	Family gatherings must be something!
Sophie:	Oh, you're right there! When it comes to events such as festivals and birthdays, we dress up, find the best presents imaginable and then wrap them magnificently – oh, it's so exciting – and we have huge parties. But there's awful pressure to do something unusual too and even more pressure from people around. For example on Rosa's third birthday . . .
Interviewer:	That's your daughter?
Sophie:	Yes . . . I made a set of puppets to put on a show for her friends from playgroup. It took me days. Immediately *their* parents asked me to put on shows for *their* children's birthdays too. And so it goes on.
Interviewer:	And is Rosa creative as well?
Sophie:	Oh, yes, she adores painting. My mother came to stay recently and I found them both in the early morning chatting away about the colour of sunrise. There they were, grandmother and granddaughter, talking about colour as if they were absolute equals.
Interviewer:	Quite an unusual topic! So let's talk about your own life a bit. I suppose you were a star student at art school –
Sophie:	Oh, you couldn't be more wrong – I was a total flop. At that time there was no interest in design. It was all introspection and gloom and doom, and I just couldn't be moulded in that way. So I took off . . .
Interviewer:	Literally?
Sophie:	Well, nothing too exotic. I went to work as a cook in a local hotel. I used to cycle there and the pay was so low that when I got a puncture I just couldn't pay for the

repair. So I offered the man in the bike shop a poster advertising his repair service, instead of money.

Interviewer: Did he accept?

Sophie: Yes – in the middle of the picture was this completely flat tyre and someone who saw it asked if he could use it to advertise a national charity bike ride.

Interviewer: That must have given you a boost!

Sophie: Yes, I had several important poster commissions after that, including some for health education. I've had some other lucky breaks too. I designed some giftwrap for a stationery company, and a woman phoned who'd been given a book wrapped in my paper. She was an author and asked me to illustrate her book of fairy stories, so that's how I got into publishing. In fact I'm just finishing a children's activity book that I've actually written and illustrated myself . . .

[pause]

tone

Now you'll hear the recording again.

[The recording is repeated.]

[pause]

That's the end of Part Three.
Now turn to Part Four.

PART 4   *Part Four*

Part Four consists of two tasks. You'll hear five short extracts in which people are talking about tourism. Look at Task One. For questions 21 to 25, choose from the list A to H each speaker's occupation. Now look at Task Two. For questions 26 to 30, choose from the list A to H each speaker's aim for the future. While you listen you must complete both tasks. You now have 45 seconds to look at Part Four.

[pause]

tone

Speaker One: Increased numbers of visitors would of course be a great benefit to the locality. My worry is though whether we have the infrastructure to cope. I'm not really concerned about the bed and breakfast sector. There's a certain amount of slack in the system. But what about transport? The railway line was removed twenty years ago and the centre gets choked up with cars as it is in the summer, all queuing to go through the narrow mediaeval gateways which are a great photo opportunity but a nightmare for through traffic. Naturally the pollution levels are rising now from traffic fumes. Reinstating the railway connection would get my vote but it won't be easy.

[pause]

Speaker Two: I think there are some wonderful places to visit around the country and it's my job to try and include them in our publications, particularly for our profitable export market. But it's all a bit piecemeal, isn't it? Take accommodation, for example. There are some pockets of excellence with great places to stay, run by friendly staff and serving interesting regional food. But you should see the pile of correspondence we receive from disappointed tourists. It's generally about the mismatch between price and quality. It's very hard to know what to recommend when we have to update our accommodation sections, especially in London. Quality across the board, that's the way forward!

[pause]

Speaker Three: Well, I think we really need to aim to try to get as many tourists as possible. But, we should start focusing on different groups. One of our key tasks has always been to gather information from overseas markets and feed it back to local tourist organisations throughout the country here so that they can develop products that suit. Currently we're thinking of marketing certain regions to the more mature, higher spending travellers who could come outside the summer holiday period, in order to extend the main tourist season. These travellers are primarily people who love historical buildings, gardens, walking and other activities which can be done in the spring and autumn.

[pause]

Speaker Four: I think tourism can bring benefits if handled wisely. One scheme which is close to my heart is the regeneration of the rural economy. By promoting traditional crafts and setting up visitor's centres to see these in action, it would be possible to go quite a long way. But we need to consider the wider issues. For instance, what means of transport are all these people going to use to get here and where are they going to stay? Can we encourage only those who do the least damage? I fear that won't happen as short-term considerations always win. People fail to understand how difficult it is to reverse damage to our surroundings.

[pause]

Speaker Five: In this business you can't stand still. We've done a lot to make the inside attractive and informative over the years, set up educational displays about everyday life five hundred years ago, redecorated the bedroom where Queen Elizabeth slept in 1570. We also restored the eighteenth-century kitchen to its former layout and we do cooking demonstrations for schoolchildren. This year it's the outside. I want to encourage families to pay to see our extended garden and zoo and the demonstrations of archery and mediaeval combat. To be profitable we really do need visitors to stay longer and spend more money in the gardens, shop and restaurant.

[pause]

Now you'll hear the recording again.

tone

[The recording is repeated.]

[pause]

That's the end of Part Four.

*There'll now be a pause of **five minutes** for you to **copy your answers onto the separate answer sheet**. Be sure to follow the numbering of all the questions. I'll remind you when there's one minute left, so that you're sure to finish in time.*

[Teacher, pause the recording here for five minutes. Remind your students when they have one minute left.]

That's the end of the test. Please stop now. Your supervisor will now collect all the question papers and answer sheets.

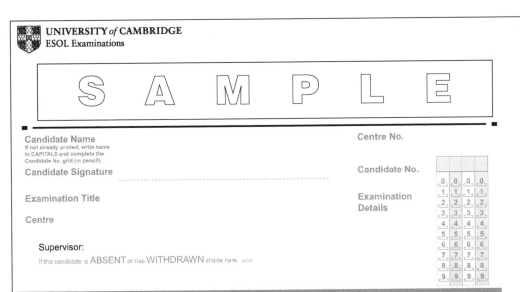

UNIVERSITY *of* CAMBRIDGE
ESOL Examinations

SAMPLE

Candidate Name
If not already printed, write name
in CAPITALS and complete the
Candidate No. grid (in pencil).

Candidate Signature

Examination Title

Centre

Supervisor:
If the candidate is ABSENT or has WITHDRAWN shade here

Centre No.

Candidate No.

**Examination
Details**

0	0	0	0
1	1	1	1
2	2	2	2
3	3	3	3
4	4	4	4
5	5	5	5
6	6	6	6
7	7	7	7
8	8	8	8
9	9	9	9

Candidate Answer Sheet

Instructions

Use a PENCIL (B or HB).

Mark ONE letter for each question.

For example, if you think B is the right answer to the question, mark your answer sheet like this:

0   A B̲ ⎯ D E F G H

Rub out any answer you wish to change using an eraser.

1	A B C D E F G H	21 A B C D E F G H
2	A B C D E F G H	22 A B C D E F G H
3	A B C D E F G H	23 A B C D E F G H
4	A B C D E F G H	24 A B C D E F G H
5	A B C D E F G H	25 A B C D E F G H
6	A B C D E F G H	26 A B C D E F G H
7	A B C D E F G H	27 A B C D E F G H
8	A B C D E F G H	28 A B C D E F G H
9	A B C D E F G H	29 A B C D E F G H
10	A B C D E F G H	30 A B C D E F G H
11	A B C D E F G H	31 A B C D E F G H
12	A B C D E F G H	32 A B C D E F G H
13	A B C D E F G H	33 A B C D E F G H
14	A B C D E F G H	34 A B C D E F G H
15	A B C D E F G H	35 A B C D E F G H
16	A B C D E F G H	36 A B C D E F G H
17	A B C D E F G H	37 A B C D E F G H
18	A B C D E F G H	38 A B C D E F G H
19	A B C D E F G H	39 A B C D E F G H
20	A B C D E F G H	40 A B C D E F G H

Sample answer sheet: Paper 3

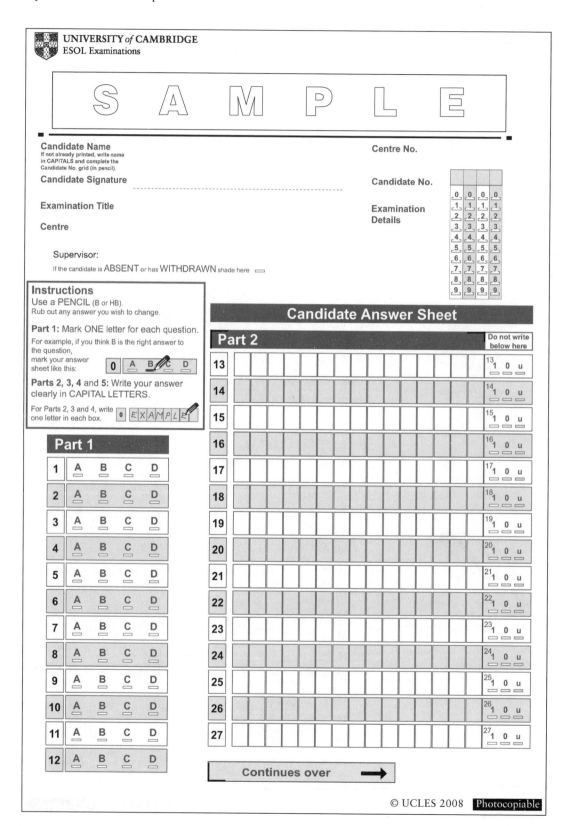

Part 3

Do not write below here

28																					28	1	0	u
29																					29	1	0	u
30																					30	1	0	u
31																					31	1	0	u
32																					32	1	0	u
33																					33	1	0	u
34																					34	1	0	u
35																					35	1	0	u
36																					36	1	0	u
37																					37	1	0	u

Part 4

Do not write below here

38																					38	1	0	u
39																					39	1	0	u
40																					40	1	0	u
41																					41	1	0	u
42																					42	1	0	u

Part 5

Do not write below here

43		43	2	1	0	u
44		44	2	1	0	u
45		45	2	1	0	u
46		46	2	1	0	u
47		47	2	1	0	u
48		48	2	1	0	u
49		49	2	1	0	u
50		50	2	1	0	u

Sample answer sheet: Paper 4

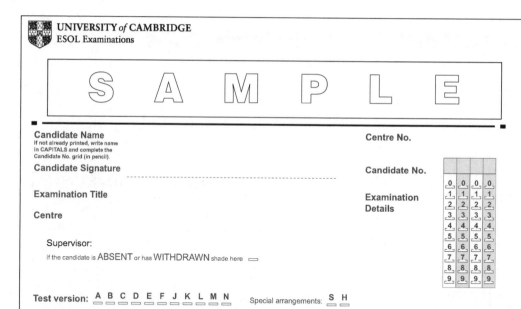

S A M P L E

Candidate Name
If not already printed, write name
in CAPITALS and complete the
Candidate No. grid (in pencil).

Candidate Signature

Examination Title

Centre

Supervisor:

If the candidate is ABSENT or has WITHDRAWN shade here ▭

Test version: A B C D E F J K L M N   Special arrangements: S H

Centre No.

Candidate No.

**Examination
Details**

0	0	0	0
1	1	1	1
2	2	2	2
3	3	3	3
4	4	4	4
5	5	5	5
6	6	6	6
7	7	7	7
8	8	8	8
9	9	9	9

Candidate Answer Sheet

Instructions

Use a PENCIL (B or HB).
Rub out any answer you wish to change using an eraser.

Parts 1, 3 and **4:**
Mark ONE letter for each question.

For example, if you think **B** is the
right answer to the question, mark
your answer sheet like this:

Part 2:
Write your answer clearly in CAPITAL LETTERS.

Write one letter or number in each box.
If the answer has more than one word, leave one
box empty between words.

For example:

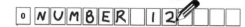

Turn this sheet over to start.

Part 1

	A	B	C
1	A	B	C
2	A	B	C
3	A	B	C
4	A	B	C
5	A	B	C
6	A	B	C

Part 2 (Remember to write in CAPITAL LETTERS or numbers)

Do not write below here

7		7 1 0 u
8		8 1 0 u
9		9 1 0 u
10		10 1 0 u
11		11 1 0 u
12		12 1 0 u
13		13 1 0 u
14		14 1 0 u

Part 3

	A	B	C	D
15	A	B	C	D
16	A	B	C	D
17	A	B	C	D
18	A	B	C	D
19	A	B	C	D
20	A	B	C	D

Part 4

	A	B	C	D	E	F	G	H
21	A	B	C	D	E	F	G	H
22	A	B	C	D	E	F	G	H
23	A	B	C	D	E	F	G	H
24	A	B	C	D	E	F	G	H
25	A	B	C	D	E	F	G	H
26	A	B	C	D	E	F	G	H
27	A	B	C	D	E	F	G	H
28	A	B	C	D	E	F	G	H
29	A	B	C	D	E	F	G	H
30	A	B	C	D	E	F	G	H